D1036456

THE MIRACLE
OF THE BREAKING

My Life, His Story. A Memoir.

THE MIRACLE OF THE BREAKING

My Life, His Story. A Memoir.

DARLENE RHODES

Niche Pressworks

Indianapolis

Dedication

I dedicate this book to my children—Joeie, Tamie, and Tiffany—who are examples of walking in Grace and Strength in spite of life's adverse situations. I'm so proud of the beautiful adult children you are today. You are great parents, and one of you is a terrific grandparent. Each of you is so kindhearted, gifted and talented, and you have used those God-given talents in your lives. I have watched you all proudly and know there are more gifts and talents to explore. You are my joy, and I know that you will never give up hoping and dreaming!

I dedicate this book to my Daddy who showed me that Grace and Forgiveness heal and never fail. I miss you Daddy, but your love and wisdom live on through your children, grandchildren and great-grandchildren because you left us a legacy to follow.

I dedicate this book to my Prince, my loving Darryl, who has shown me Grace in his life and how to accept it in mine. Thank you for seeing the gifts inside of me and nudging me to tell "His Story" around the world. What a beautiful journey of life we are on! Thank you for two beautiful daughters, Chris and Elesha, who on their own, from "the beginning of us," have called me "Mom." Their love and laughter truly captured my heart. I am a richly blessed woman.

Most of all, I dedicate this book to the Lover of my soul, my Master, my Redeemer, my Savior, my Lord and my Jesus. You have loved me unconditionally and held me close in every storm of life. Forever, I am honored to be Your daughter, Your storyteller.

Acknowledgements

The inspiration to write this book has come from many encouragers and the silent voices who have walked paths similar to my story.

I am so grateful to my Chief Editor Holly Deherrera, an excellent author, whose expertise breathed life into this work and who I am honored to call my friend. Many thanks to Debbie Allen, a great editor who read my manuscript and offered valuable insight to details. I'm grateful to my friend David, an author who kept giving me thumbs up. I am very grateful for my daughter Tiffany for reading my many rewrites and helping with grammatical errors. I am especially indebted to my *Women Around the World* team, Tiffany, Missy, Sarah, Kristi, Carrisa and Dara, who spend hours planning for ladies' conferences and who are my constant warriors in encouragement and prayers. And thank you, Nicole, for your amazing skills and pushing me beyond what I could see!

>

Contents

Table of Contents

Chapter 1

A Bug on a Board

Salem, Missouri

We all sat around the dining room table while Mom slammed cabinets and slid the dishes—with little flowered edges the color of the inside of an avocado—onto the dark wood.

"Why not come sit down and join us, Audrey?" Daddy said, his voice as soft as a bunny's ear.

I shifted in my seat, my legs not quite long enough to let my feet hit the floor and wished that maybe I lived at the neighbor girl's house just down the street, 'cause I bet her Mom didn't carry on near as much as mine did.

Then Mom got in a huff (she was always getting in huffs) and said, "You know good and well I said earlier today I wanted fish for dinner." She looked at Daddy like he was a bug, and she was pinning him on a board.

"Well, goodness, Audrey, I didn't know it was so very important to you to have fish." Daddy sat with his hands spread out over the edge of the table, the skin under his nails going from pink to white. "I'll go now if you care so much."

"It's too late now," she mumbled, crossing her arms over her chest, from her standing position near the kitchen.

I wondered, if it *was* too late, how come she said anything in the first place. But I swallowed the words down.

"Well, then, join us to eat. No point in wasting a perfectly good meal with all this fussing."

I looked over at my brother, Paul, who had obviously given up on Mom coming to the table and was shoveling in a mouthful of beans, ignoring the whole mess.

"I will not be joining you, Luther. I'm not hungry anymore." She said each word louder than the last.

At that, Daddy stood to his full height, tall like a tree, his napkin sliding to the ground. He snatched his keys off the counter and walked out the door, shaking his head. "Always making such a fuss over nothing." The screen door snapped shut behind him, and I held my breath as I listened for his car to start up.

Mom walked over to the table and leaned in to face me, her arms bent and her brown curls like a frame around her face, and said through her teeth, "You tell your daddy that if he leaves, I'll be gone when he gets back." I felt as small as an ant when she looked at me like that. My heart thumped like fingers on the keys of a church organ, and I swallowed a stinging lump, trying to keep from crying like a baby. *Just 'cause I'm five doesn't mean I can't be brave.*

My tummy felt like a scramble of knots all pulling in different directions. I jumped up, bumping my knee against the table, and ran out the front door. I yelled and yelled to Daddy, who had pulled the car out of the gravel driveway and was starting off down the road, the tires crunching as he rolled slowly along. I ran and ran, my bare feet slapping against the pavement, screaming, "Daddy! Daddy!"

He slowed the car and then stopped. I tugged open the front door and climbed into the big seat by Daddy, tears falling free as the mulberry blossoms in springtime. "What is it, Sugarfoot?" he asked. He leaned toward me, the soft skin between his eyes bunching up in a pile and wiped at my face with his big hand.

I took in a deep breath and said between gasps, "Mom says she'll be gone when you get back. You can't go!" I would do most anything to keep Daddy from being hurt. He didn't deserve it. He'd never hurt a flea. All the time Mom sent me off to do things she didn't want to do. *Tell your daddy this. Tell your daddy that.* Only I didn't want to tell daddy the things she said.

Rubbing a hand up and down my arm, he spoke in his sweet way. "It'll be alright, Darlene." His brown eyes looked sad behind his black-frame glasses, and he pressed his lips together like he might just say something else but didn't want to. Then he backed up the car and turned into the driveway in front of our house, which looked like a white sugar cube. Daddy twisted the key, making the humming sound stop, and got out and walked around to get me from my side. He lifted me from the seat and held me close to his chest as he walked slowly, steadily into the house where Mom was nowhere to be found. But that was fine with me. I knew she'd gone off to her room to be mad. At least Daddy was home. We could sit down and eat the food Mom made but wouldn't eat, and everything would be okay.

It was just Mom and Daddy, Paul, Shirley and me in the house. The older ones were gone: Faye and Don and Leon. Shirley would be getting married soon, she told me, but until then she tucked me inside her bed every night, and we snuggled up. I felt safe as a bear in a den with her.

I loved Daddy taking me along on his trips to visit people and pray or to offer a kind word. We'd bump along in his car, as big as a boat, and talk and laugh. He'd tell me about the times when I was itty bitty, and I'd sing in front of the church with him holding me in a standing position on the pulpit. "You sounded just like a baby angel." I liked thinking about those times. They made the sad part in me feel more like sunshine.

Chapter 2

Mulberry Tree Days

Salem, Missouri

I set my bare foot on the rough wood of the mulberry tree out in our front yard in Salem, Missouri, then pulled myself up to my most favorite spot in the middle, where I could sit and be covered in a whole bunch of tear-shaped, green leaves, hidden in the center of a big old cocoon. Inside, the sunshine glittered in through the canopy and I sat back, one leg dangling and one stretched out long on the branch, as I snatched at the fruit that looked like bruised raspberries, the juices staining my hands and the front of my dress. The mulberry tree was my place—my place to think on things and my place to pretend everything would be okay, even though my tummy hurt so much that sometimes I thought I might be sick.

I got scared a lot ... loud barking dogs, big boys on the street with spinning bicycles, and Mom, her loud voice and angry looks that cut through my tender heart like a knife. I was mostly scared of being *the reason* for her anger. Mom didn't like lots of things. She didn't even like Daddy's job as the preacher. Sometimes, I could sense her stiffening rigidly right in the middle of service. *I couldn't understand it.* He ever lives in my memories ... his brown slacks, white button-up shirt, and suspenders, preaching from the Good Book. Daddy was the smartest, nicest man who ever lived and breathed, but I just knew he'd say *something* in his sermon that would irritate her. I didn't see what he could possibly have said to make her spit fire.

One Saturday afternoon, Paul, Mom, Daddy and I drove along in the white Mercury heading to Grandma's and Grandpa's house for the day. The hot day felt like a million-pound blanket, and our white car, a big old tin can, sizzled us inside. The rains from the past few days made everything green as a caterpillar and squishy, too.

Daddy looked over his shoulder at me, lifting his eyebrows high and said, "Think we should do it, Sugarfoot?" He pulled up to Sinkin' Creek, the place that had only just a little bit of river, and where sometimes we'd drive our car across, like Jesus walking on water.

I nodded, bouncing in my seat.

"This'll be fun, won't it?" Daddy asked, his face grinning through the mirror, pointing backward at Paul and me.

Daddy pulled the car forward, inching into the creek like a cottonmouth looking for food. Paul and I giggled. The rains had made the water a little higher than usual, and I wondered if we'd float right on down the river like a canoe. Instead, the car rumbled into the flowing water, most of the way across the creek, then stopped.

Words flew out of Mom's mouth like stones out of a slingshot. "Luther, I knew this would happen. Now we're gonna be too late for seeing my parents. You've ruined the whole day with your foolishness! You knew better than to go this way. You knew the creek would be up. You knew this would take us longer to get there!" She kept yelling like she had a whole pile of words she'd stored up for just such a disaster. She twisted around and glared at me when Daddy got out of the car to look under the round hood. I stared down at my hands and twisted the fabric of my dress into a tight little ball.

It's my fault. It's all my fault, I thought to myself. Daddy's head disappeared behind the lid of the car and I wondered how I could make it right. I swallowed the hot lump in my throat and squeezed my eyes shut. *I'll help fix it. This is all my fault. He did this, so I could have fun. Now look what happened.* So, I grabbed an old towel from the back seat and climbed out, the warm water of the creek reaching up to the middle of my legs, my skirt floating around my waist. Beside Daddy, I pressed the towel against the hot metal of the engine, letting my tears fall now that Mom couldn't see. "I'm so sorry, Daddy. I'm so sorry."

And he looked over at me, resting a hand over mine, leaning toward me so his eyes, the color of the sand near the creek bank, were close to mine, and said, "It's not your fault, Darlene. Don't worry. It'll be alright. It's not that big a deal. Besides," he pressed the towel down into the place with all the hoses. "It was fun, wasn't it?"

Later, the car started up and we drove the rest of the way across the creek. We went to Grandma and Grandpa's and Mom calmed down. But, inside something felt wrong. I knew that nothing I said or did and nothing Daddy said or did would ever bring a bright smile to Mom's face or make her love me right. Seemed like she just didn't know how.

And a little aching feeling, one that made me feel small and afraid and a little lonely all at the same time, built a tiny little house in my chest, one that looked nothing like the inside of that mulberry tree.

Chapter 3

Mom Wore a Flowered Dress

Salem, Missouri

Christmas morning came, and I tiptoed down the steps with Paul in front of me. Each stair squeaked like it was telling on us. But there was no need because when we rounded the corner into the living room where the pretty green tree stood in the corner all lit up with fat red, green, and blue bulbs, Mom and Daddy stood nearby, as if they'd been waiting. Mom wore a flowered dress and a rare smile, and Daddy grinned like he might burst if we didn't come in and sit down around the tree. And that's when I spotted her: a pretty doll, as big as a real-life baby, sitting in the tree. I ran forward and grabbed her, pulling her little face up against mine, studying her small pink mouth, shaped in an 'O' and her round eyes the color of the sky. And I kissed her plastic face, smiling, loving her so much—especially because of Mom standing beside Daddy. Especially because it meant they loved me. Both of them.

Chapter 4

Church in the Yard

Salem, Missouri

Summer rolled into Salem, like a train on big wheels. Paul and I played on the sawdust piles made at the sawmill near our home. We ran up to the top, our feet pressing steps into the soft mountain, and then sat on the tippy top, looking across the world. On those days, we were like a king and queen looking out over our kingdom.

And on other days, we congregated in the yard, and Paul was the preacher, calling down fire and brimstone on my niece and me—two tiny church ladies, sitting cross-legged in the backyard with the tickly grass underneath us. My big brother would stalk back and forth, yelling for us to "Repent!" My niece and I giggled behind our hands when Paul gave us a dark, angry look, reminding us to stay on the "straight and narrow path." We'd just look at each other and shrug, not sure what any of it meant, but thinking Paul's bright red face and the sweat he kept wiping away with the back of his hand, was funny.

My feet looked like a bouquet of peachy flowers, free of socks and pinchy shoes, sprouting in front of my short legs, dancing and waving in the muggy air. I wriggled them as Paul preached, and I watched a butterfly darting and landing nearby.

Sometimes we'd walk a few blocks to the dime store and buy sweets with change bouncing in our pockets from Daddy, feeling grown up and rich. Those were happy days. Free days. Sunshiny days.

But summertime doesn't last forever.

Chapter 5

A Queen with No Crown

Salem, Missouri

The itchy, black of a mourning dress replaced the flowery yellow one I often wore—the one Daddy liked me to wear because he said it made my eyes look pretty. At nine, and all grown up, I helped to prepare things for Uncle Melvin's wake, right in the living room of my Aunt Rosie's house. Every room felt grey-gloomy and everyone spoke in whispers as if talking normally would mean we weren't sad enough.

My sixteen-year-old cousin, Lenny, elbowed me. "Come help me get chairs from the shed."

We walked out the door, around the side of the house, everyone busy making food and fixing things just right inside. He nudged me into the dark space and the creepy crawly feeling of fear danced down my spine. *Stop being such a chicken about everything.* I squared my shoulders, telling myself that I didn't need to be afraid.

Lenny leaned toward me, his chocolatey brown eyes searching mine.

He offered a smile that looked halfway between mean and friendly. "Let's do something now. It'll help me feel better." He angled his head back toward the house, so I knew he meant about his own daddy, lying dead in the living room. He raised his eyebrows and told me that he needed me to touch him in his private places. I stood as still as a statue, as still as a queen on top of a mountain, looking out over her land. I pretended I wasn't in that shed and that my cousin wasn't telling me to take down my panties, too, because I knew that was my private place, and it wasn't supposed to be shared with cousins in sheds. A black snake of burning shame worked its way through my chest, kept my mouth from working, kept me from saying anything. He just did his own thing, and I stayed there feeling so much smaller than him and feeling so dirty it was like I'd rolled in mud. Only not the nice soft kind, but the kind with pokey stones all through it, making me bleed. After that, he snatched a stack of chairs and left. But he turned and said over his shoulder in a near growl, "If you say a word, you'll be sorry." My skin prickled, wondering how it could get worse. How could I be *more* sorry than I already was?

Whenever we visited as a family, Lenny would find a way, when nobody was looking, to shove a large hand down my pants or up my shirt, quick as a lizard hiding from the sun. *This is all my fault. If I'd only run away that first time. If I'd only screamed and run to Daddy, he'd have saved me, and Lenny would have been in big trouble and then he'd leave me alone.* But I didn't and because I wasn't brave, it was my fault. Lenny knew I was as weak as a queen with no crown at all.

REFLECTIONS:
STORMS AND FOREIGN LANDS

*Y*ou're flying so high above the earth you can see the curve of the globe and your destination is somewhere beyond the horizon of blue-black meeting blue-brown. It's hard to tell from here that your gauge is one degree off. You just keep flying, mind wandering to all the things you wish weren't happening in your life. You keep thinking that if only that one thing hadn't failed—you keep thinking if you hadn't failed so miserably, you might be in a different place. And the miles stretch and stretch, and that one degree tilts the plane further and further from the mark.

One little degree. Not so much. But enough to plummet your plane into the South Sea instead of the soft landing on soft sand you hoped for.

I got off course one degree at a time, and, before I knew it, I was in a sea of pain and couldn't find my way to the warbling circle of sunshine from my place in the abyssal zone of deep sorrow. *How did I get here? I should have known better. I should have seen it.* I wallowed there. I lingered because I didn't look at the promised hope above. I lingered because of shame.

The pain heaped on my head, pinning me, thousands of pounds immobilizing me. But then I yelled for Him. I called His name. I called, and He came, His gentle hand reaching for me, telling me, "This way. I'm here. Stay close to <u>My</u> side. I'll do something amazing, just watch. And don't let go of <u>My</u> hand."

The Miracle Worker is here.

He's standing on the surface of the sea and calling your name.

Chapter 6

Fear Turns
into Adventure

Piedmont, Missouri

The cold morning made the streets look as shiny as glass. Still, Daddy made a promise to pick up a man from the church, and he wasn't one to go back on his word. So, we set out, Daddy and I, in the Mercury, into the world with the trees looking like they were covered in crushed glass. I pressed my face to the window, feeling like it was a fairy world. My hands spread out on the cold frost made by my breath being so hot and the world outside being so freezing. Missouri didn't get much crushed-glass weather.

The car puttered along. Seemed like it wasn't used to the cold either because it seemed to hiccup and cough and then stopped, dead as a doornail, right there in the very middle of the street. Daddy said, "Hmm. That's not good, is it Sugarfoot?"

I shook my head, my stomach tight as a bag full of rocks, all of a sudden. "What're you gonna do, Daddy?"

He twisted the key and pumped his foot up and down on the pedal and the car only made a whole bunch of noise but never did start to rumble like usual. "Well, Darlene, let's just hope some kind soul comes along to give us a ride."

Before he finished his sentence one of our neighbors drove past our car and parked in front of us, then jumped out of his pickup and kneeled a little to look in the driver window. "Got a problem, Pastor?"

"In fact, I do. Car just up and died."

"Died?"

"Died."

I twisted my dress in my hands, not liking the word "died." How come they had to keep saying that word?

"I've got a tow chain," the man said. "I maybe could pull you home."

Daddy nodded like it was the best idea and grinned. "Sounds like it just might work." Then he climbed out of the car and slammed the door shut against the wind.

The two men worked together, making a whole bunch of clunking noises with a fat chain, and I sat in the car alone, listening to their mumbly voices, wishing I was home because the car was getting colder and colder. I pulled my knees up to my chest and snatched my dress down over them, then wrapped my arms around my nubby legs. After what felt like two zillion years, Daddy got in and pulled the bar until it said, "N," and the neighbor started driving. Then it was like we were on a sled, Daddy and I, dragged behind the big truck in front. The icy road made the truck and us move around, like we were two fish on one big long line instead of two cars held together by a giant chain.

The Mercury squirmed back and forth and Daddy's leg danced up and down—I wondered what he was trying to do—all while the back of the truck seemed like it would swallow up the front of our car with one gulp.

I skootched down, not wanting to see when our car hit the truck. It was plain to see that the road was not wanting us to stop, just to skate around.

When we finally got to the house, still being dragged behind like we were being delivered by a milkman, Daddy turned around to me and grinned, the lines around his mouth and the squinty lines beside his eyes going deeper. "That was an adventure, if I've ever had one." And he started to laugh. "I was sure we'd kiss the back of that truck, but somehow we missed it. Kind of fun, though, wasn't it?"

I nodded and all the worry that I had kept knotted inside came out in a belly laugh, letting out the pressure like the top of a soda bottle. Daddy and I stayed like that for a while just laughing and wiping away smiling-tears. And I knew that with Daddy, even the scariest things, could be adventures. Even problems could become happy memories.

Chapter 7

Daddy Kneeling
at the Altar

Piedmont, Missouri

Music took away some of the sadness that had planted itself inside me and grown as fat as a tree. I walked into the cool dark of the church that was next to our house, and I sat down at the piano, letting my fingers say the words and breathe out the ache. In those times, I remembered about Jesus and His love for me. I believed it because Daddy told me so, and he never lied. I remembered that no matter how bad a girl I was—letting big boys do bad things with me, or causing trouble that made Mom's face get as dark as a coloring book covered in black crayon—that Jesus died on a cross to tell me He forgave me. Sometimes, when I was alone playing pretty music, I cried too. Mostly because, even though Daddy loved me and Jesus loved me, I couldn't see how I would ever be brave enough to do anything good with my life. I felt so small and weak, like a teeny-tiny mouse in a big, metal trap.

The morning sounds hadn't started yet—just Dad, making a racket, as was his usual way even when trying his very best to be quiet. I lay in my bed, my room as dark as velvet, listening to his shuffling, liking the familiar sound of him getting ready for the day and heading off to the church to pray. I glanced over at the small, black-faced clock, the glowing arms saying it was 4:00. I tiptoed out, my jammies hanging nearly to the ground, so I lifted them with my fingertips and made my way down the steps to just see what Daddy would do, even though it was always the same. I left the parsonage and my feet slapped on the short gravel path to the church, then I slipped inside and perched my bottom in the back pew, leaning on the wooden seat in front, my chin leaning on my hands.

Daddy kneeled at the old wooden altar at the front, his back to me, crisscrossed with suspenders. And he talked into the large room, his head bowed as if he spoke to his best friend.

"Dear Lord, bless my family," he said. Then he went through each and every one of us. "Bless my wife. You know her struggles. You know her hurts. Minister to her, Jesus." I wished Mom knew about Daddy's words. Wished she would hear and be satisfied instead of the constant complaints she always voiced that sounded like nails on a shiny chalkboard. Daddy spent some time praying for Paul and the other grown kids.

"And bless Darlene, Lord." A fat lump filled my throat because Daddy said my name so sweetly I knew his love in the way he said it. "You know what is going on in her life right now, and You know what she needs. I pray that You bring her peace and comfort." I felt hot tears fill my eyes, making the picture of my daddy, praying on the hard floor for *me*, look wobbly and blurry.

I skootched out of the pew and quietly left, running across the small, rocky parking lot, to the house, up the stairs, then crawled back into my bed.

REFLECTIONS:
TIRED AND NEEDING REST

The apostles gathered around Jesus and reported to him all they had done and taught. Then, because so many people were coming and going that they did not even have a chance to eat, he said to them, "Come with me by yourselves to a quiet place and get some rest."

—Mark 6:30-31

They were tired, the disciples and Jesus. Days and days of ministering in the hot, Galilean sunshine. Just one more person needing help. Just one more smile, one more kind word.

Are you tired? Do you feel your strength floating off like a cloud over a dry, desert land? Jesus invites us to come with Him to a quiet place and rest. But that requires movement—from us—in His direction, movement away from the problems that nearly bury us alive. Away from the shame, fatigue, anxiety, sorrow, disillusionment, helplessness, anger and fear toward Him. Jesus! The giver of life. The Miracle Worker.

He's calling. He's waiting. Take those steps away from the throng and stress toward the hope and life and joy He wants to offer. Those are only found in His presence, only found by spending time with Him. Time enough to calm the other voices and to hear His. Space enough to separate from the imminent to the transcendent.

Jesus waits, hand outstretched to ours and smiles. He says, "Come and rest with Me." Just like Daddy took time with his Lord, we are invited to do the same.

He calls. *I love you, and I want to minister to your heart. You matter that much to me.*

Chapter 8

Mom with a Gun

Fredericktown, Missouri

Mom made the outfits: four matching A-line dresses, with a swarm of blue flowers. We all stood together, my friends and I, shoulder to shoulder. We'd driven an hour in Mom and Daddy's vehicle up to the Cape Girardeau television station. The Harmonettes, as we called ourselves, had been invited to sing before a live studio audience. So, we did, with our puffy curled up bangs and a smile. I looked out to where my parents sat, proud as two hens watching their chick grow feathers—even Mom grinned and laughed and clapped. And we sang our four-part harmonies to a clunky camera, voicing praises to God.

Nights often found our singing group in my living room, weaving harmony to Paul's guitar, with me on the old upright piano.

"How about *Wouldn't Take Nothing for My Journey Now?*" Mom said from her perch on the easy chair, off and to the side of where us girls huddled. The words lifted the quiet of the room, spoke some of my hidden sorrow.

"I've had a lot of heartaches met a lot of grief and woe. And when I would stumble then I would humble down. And there I would say thank the Lord."

I looked over at Mom, sitting in her spot in the corner, head resting back, arms draped down and hands resting on her legs, her eyes closed and the normal scrunched brow, relaxed. *What's she thinking? Would she change anything about her life? Did she wish it different?*

And I wondered about her for the millionth time—wondered where the unsettledness came from. Did she share those places with Jesus once? Did she ever truly know His closeness? Why the sadness? Why the heartsickness? Why the words that rattled out in anger so often?

But, for that moment, in that little living room with us girls and Paul raising our words to the sky, we sang, and she listened—letting the words soothe something deep inside, and she was at peace.

But, also woven in were signs that something inside Mom was broken. I stepped into the house, stacking my armful of school books on the kitchen table. Mom didn't look up and offer a greeting or ask about my day, just stood in the kitchen, silent as stone, stirring a pot, like she was a robot emptied out of feeling.

Sometimes she'd step away from what she'd been fixing, walk back to her room and click the door shut. The smell of something burning would greet Daddy as he entered the house. And just as if it were as natural as breathing, he moved into where Mom had been standing and removed the scalded pot of food, set it under the faucet to fill with water, and started dinner again fresh.

One afternoon, we all worked out in the yard, the sunshine lifting the wet off the clothing we'd washed and wrung out. Then we clipped the pile onto a long clothesline. Mom stood to the side, arms crossed over her plump middle, and scowled. Something had gotten her riled and Daddy had just been on the receiving end of her tirade until he'd ended it with a gentle, "That's enough, Audrey."

After that, she refused to help, but wouldn't do everyone the favor of just leaving. No, that wouldn't make her point. That wouldn't be enough punishment.

Hot anger made my cheeks flush, and I spoke under my breath to Daddy, who cranked the handle of the wringer. "Why do you put up with it? How come you just stay with her no matter what?"

Daddy stopped his work, looked at me, his eyes full of understanding but also a deep-down strength and said, "She's my wife, Darlene."

Daddy wasn't home that day. Neither was Paul. The house felt like a goosebump kind of quiet. I walked from the living room, through the kitchen, then turned back and walked to Mom and Daddy's room. The space was empty and silent except for the tick-tick-tick of the clock perched on their side table.

"Mom?" I said.

Quiet.

The bathroom door was shut, and I tried the handle. Locked. "Mom?"

I heard her shuffling like she scooched across the floor on her bottom. "Leave, Darlene!" Her voice jarred against the lack of noise.

"Why? What's wrong, Mom?"

"Just leave. You shouldn't be here!" She sounded strangled and high-pitched.

I pressed an ear to the wood, trying to determine something, anything, to help me understand what was going on. "Why are you in there? What's wrong?"

Mom growled out, "Because I wanna die!" I could hear the silent sobs through the wall. *Through me.* Hands rubbing against the wooden framing. Her head thunking against the door, a sad beat.

I jiggled the handle. "Don't say that!" I pushed my shoulder against the door. "You shouldn't say that, Mom!"

She screamed, "I'm gonna blow my brains out! I will! I don't want to live anymore!"

That's when I realized ... Mom must have snatched the shotgun daddy used for hunting, then locked herself into the tiny room.

Acid filled my throat. "No, no, no. Please, Mom! Please!" I pictured the linoleum covered in Mom's blood. Pictured her face, slack and without life. "Please, Mom!" I pounded my fist on the door, the action stinging against my skin.

But she didn't listen. Or at least she didn't respond. The silence resumed. I sank down, head leaning against the door, hands splayed out like fans, listening and praying that my poor, sick Mom wouldn't take her life this day.

Mom lived, but the shroud of darkness she carried never lifted. The ache of some ancient hurt never left her eyes, and she never wasted words on trivial kindnesses. She and Daddy were like sunrise is to sunset that way—he threw away love like he had an endless supply. It was like Mom didn't have near enough even to bring a smile or to pull me into a hug. It was like she had no clue how to fill up with the love only Jesus could give—so it could spill out on others.

At church, I stood, so many Sundays, tears pouring down my face, singing to God. Telling Him about the sadness, telling Him about that terrible day when Mom nearly left forever. And I knew He heard. He listened and cried with me and reminded me over and over again, like waves lapping against my legs, of His love. His love, that I knew soaked through me and in me, trying to heal the hurt spots—telling me that I belonged to Him no matter what. Come what may.

Chapter 9

Weakness and Vows

Salem, Missouri

Daddy pastored the faithful folks who attended his church, which now stood over the place our old basement had been. At Sunday night service during my freshman year of high school, I met Joe. Tall with hair the color of sand, all slicked back on the sides and loose and dangerous in the middle, with eyes that seemed to dance with some secret glee.

"Hi," he said as he reached a large hand out and I offered mine back, swallowed up from that first greeting by his pull. "I'm Joe." He grinned and waited for my reply.

"Darlene," I said, less confident than I'd intended. I wanted my glow to match his, but it couldn't. I cleared my throat. "Darlene Hassell. My daddy's the pastor."

He glanced over his shoulder to where my dad stood, shaking the hands of parishioners, his voice offering a kind word to each one, bold and loud enough for us to hear.

"Well, it is nice to meet you, Pastor's Daughter." And he winked.

When he left, the room felt a fraction darker, like the bulbs had been reduced to a lower wattage.

Joe began attending Daddy's church regularly with his mom, a devout woman, full of Jesus. I found out that Joe didn't have that though, hadn't ever offered his life to the Lord. Still, that didn't stop me from being drawn to him.

"Can I take you out sometime? Maybe we could grab a burger or something." Again, with the smile that lit my insides on fire.

"I'd like that," I said, my face feeling like I'd warmed it in front of a campfire.

Joe picked me up in his '54 Ford, since he was 16 and able to drive. I felt taller and more womanly sitting there beside him, his hand hooked over the steering wheel, talking away as he drove, like he hadn't a care in the world. I wondered if he knew I wasn't even quite 15. I sat up straighter and crossed my hands over my knees, listening as he talked all about his daddy's logging business, about his crazy brothers who lived crazy lives, and about how he wanted to be different. He wanted to be his own man.

I watched his profile as he spoke, watched his smile and decided something new was happening in me. And I sank into the feeling, like the oven warming a batch of fresh cookie dough. He turned to me, his eyebrows bunching a little in the middle.

"I like you, Darlene. Thanks for listening to me carrying on." He looked out the front windshield at the road as he drove, then snatched a glance at me. "I like you a lot."

I nodded, "I like you too, Joe."

After that, the only sound was that of the engine and the tires humming on the road and my chest thumping, scared and excited all at once. Joe drove past the courthouse and past the music store, onto the drag where friends parked and chatted and laughed too loud. He honked his horn and waved his free arm out the window, and the people we passed yelled, "Hi, Joe!"

And I was a part of it. Grown up and included in his circle now. In his light, I felt brighter too.

Time smoothed by and soothed old aches, pushed back by Joe's attentiveness and presence. We were "together" exclusively and had been dating for nearly a year.

He pulled into an overlook, killed the engine and the headlights, and just sat there, staring out over the small town of Salem, lights dotting the horizon. The wind whispered in through the window, rolled down all the way. I spread my hand into the breeze, feeling the tickle, enjoying the peace.

Joe turned to me, the darkness shadowing his face, but not so much I couldn't see the features I'd grown to love. "You're so beautiful." He ran his hand down my hair. "I love you." And he leaned in, pressing his mouth to mine. His hands worked up into the back of my hair, softly at first but as we kissed, they seemed to pull tighter, urgency defining his movements. He allowed his hands to wander and I pulled back and shook my head.

"We can't, Joe. We've talked about this."

"Please," he whispered.

Everything in me pulled in opposite directions. Half of me longing to offer everything to Joe and the other half remembering a lifetime of teaching spoken in my father's voice–Bible words that I knew to be timeless–about being careful and not sharing too much before marriage and keeping pure before the all-seeing, all-knowing, but still all-loving Father in heaven.

"I just can't," I said even as Joe's breath danced down my neck, weakening my resolve. He pulled back, a dark cloud slipping between us.

He turned away, twisted the key in the ignition, the engine roaring against the quiet as he peeled out of our spot, taking me home to the deafening music of his disappointment.

The next night his mom called. "Darlene, Joe went out tonight." She paused. "With his brother and his wife and Trudy." I knew about her. Knew about her reputation to do all the things I'd told Joe I wouldn't do. *Maybe if I hadn't pushed him away he wouldn't have chosen to go out with someone like her.* "Darlene, you don't deserve to be treated this way. You deserve better." She ended with, "I just thought you should know."

The next time Joe and I were together it was as if nothing had taken place. That he hadn't left me, his anger filling the cab of the car. That he hadn't gone out with a girl with loose morals. And he kept pressing for me to sleep with him.

The scene repeated over and over, my "no" getting less firm, less sure. *Give him what he wants. You're lucky to have him. He'll go back to someone like Trudy if you don't just say yes.* And finally, when he pressed again, hands roaming, mouth whispering words of love in my ear, I allowed it. I allowed him to be a part of my being and, even while it was happening, I knew it was wrong. Tears wanted to come out, and my throat ached like I'd been punched.

Afterward, Joe stroked my hair back from my face and told me it was okay. That he loved me, and he'd never hurt me. And I believed him.

34

Daddy always took me to the doctor for my female issues. Being anemic, I was used to my sporadic cycle, to the weakness and discomfort. So, when I felt the room spin whenever I stood, black spots and glitter dotting my vision, I knew I needed to see the doctor. Maybe the iron pills weren't working, and my blood counts were low.

I sat on the exam bed, the paper liner making a crinkly sound as I shifted. My doctor had done the normal blood draw, and I'd waited, uncomfortable, the silence of the room broken only by a small wall clock offering a small, tick, tick, tick.

The doctor sat across from me in his rolling chair, looked down at his hands, then up, his eyes showing some regret or maybe concern. "Darlene, you're pregnant."

Prickles dotted my lips, down my neck, skittered across my shoulders and down to my fingers. *Oh, Jesus, no. What do I do, what do I do?* I shook my head, my eyes glued to the floor, to a spot on the tile that seemed to warp and move in a blob. The room filled with white, blurring out the walls and the equipment perched along a counter, blurring out my hands knotting my shirt in a ball as if they were unattached. *Jesus, help me.* Tears burned against my throat. I shook my head again. No. It's not true. *I can't be pregnant.*

The doctor's voice sounded like it came from the end of a million-mile tunnel. "Darlene, do you want me to go talk to your dad?"

I still couldn't look at him because I felt like a dirty rag running over a wet car engine. *This is all your fault. You're such a weakling.* I managed a nod, and he left. His shoes retreated through the crack of the door, then it closed, and silence swallowed up a sob I couldn't hold in any longer.

The door opened. Shoes squeaked on the floor. Warm hands squeezed my shoulders and Daddy's voice said, "We'll get through this." And then I hunched forward, my cries tumbling out now.

"I'm so sorry, Daddy. I'm so sorry." I knew the shame I'd created. Knew as the pastor, people expected more from him—from his daughter. Knew he must be holding in his disappointment like a wall holding back a flash flood.

But he only prayed and rubbed my back and said again and again, "We'll get through this. We'll get through this."

On the drive home, I said, "Mom's going to kill me." I pictured her face pinched in disappointment. The scowl. The look of suspicion like I'd planned it all along. "I don't know what we're gonna do." I said "we" because I knew deep inside my chest, deep in the hidden space that held that tiny flash of light, that Daddy was in this with me.

The car angled off the street, wheels crunching on asphalt, pulling in front of the big old Baptist church on McArthur street. Daddy turned to me. "Darlene, we have to do what's right here. We need to tell Joe and his parents. Then you stay with them and I will talk to your mom." His voice calmed the rattle in my chest, in my throat, the tears that were conjured from the mere thought of the anger Mom would unleash.

The drive to Joe's home on the outskirts of town seemed to take forever but finally we pulled into his driveway. We stepped into Joe's house, his daddy sitting in the overstuffed recliner, his sweet mom standing in the living room with an apron over her dress, and Joe with his hands in his pockets looking back and forth between Daddy and me, like he could decipher the riddle that way.

I cleared my throat and looked over at Joe. "I'm pregnant." Quiet. Quiet as a tomb. Quiet as fear.

Joe stepped forward like he wanted to touch me, then dropped his hand like he realized that's what got us into this mess in the first place. His dad didn't move, didn't speak. But his mom moved to me, offering a hug.

Daddy said to Joe, "I didn't come here to say I want you to marry my daughter. We just wanted to do what's right."

Joe's mom said, "We're going to have a little Joe," as if she'd been holding in the joy the news brought, instead of the shame I'd expected.

"Of course, I want to marry her," Joe said, like he'd been stunned and took a moment to snap out of it. "Of course, I want this baby."

Daddy nodded and then quietly left to face Mom.

Hours later, Joe pulled into our drive. I got out and then stepped into the house. Mom and Daddy were there in the living room. She was a cloud without rain, he was the sun. She stood and glared, hands clenched in balls.

"How could you do this to me? How could you bring such shame on this family?" She stepped forward, her voice rising like a storm. "Why?!" she screamed. "Why would you do something so belittling?!"

Daddy stepped between us, a shield guarding against a pummeling of hail. He turned to Mom. "Enough. Don't mark our grandchild with your angry words."

In that moment, I knew the Grace-filled love of the Lord more than ever before. I knew it in the set of Daddy's jaw. His blocking me from her. The love despite my failure. And, I knew that he loved my baby even more than I did yet. Already, he loved. Sight unseen. A burning filled my chest. A returned love so fierce that it filled my eyes with tears and my insides with the knowledge that with him by my side, nothing could break me apart. Not even Mom.

Joe and I married a month later. Daddy did the ceremony and only a few family members attended. Mom rallied and took me to get a white, knee-length dress and a small veil. So I stood there, skinny and not showing but still feeling sure everyone knew. I'd dropped out of school at just fifteen, so why wouldn't they?

God, how can you ever use me now? I'm nothing. And I'm so full of sorrow at grieving You. I'm full of weakness. And full to the brim with fear. How can You ever use someone like me? How?

REFLECTIONS: CROWDS, DESPERATE FOR JESUS

So, they went away by themselves in a boat to a solitary place. But many who saw them leaving recognized them and ran on foot from all the towns and got there ahead of them. When Jesus landed and saw a large crowd, he had compassion on them, because they were like sheep without a shepherd. So, he began teaching them many things.

—MARK 6:32-34

*D*esperate people do desperate things. On this day in a town near the Sea of Galilee, word had gotten out. Jesus was there, and He was healing people. Crowds gathered around Jesus, like a sick man needing a cure. These people, from all walks of life, followed Jesus, and they followed the disciples to see what would happen!

And even though Jesus and His disciples were almost too tired to function, the Savior had compassion. When He looked on that clog of humanity, He didn't see a blur of color. He saw the faces, the lines of worry, the bunching of skin between the eyes and He saw inside, too. He saw the troubles, the pain, and He couldn't resist. He wouldn't turn them down.

He never turns a seeking soul down. It's why He came in the first place. In the middle of my shame, Jesus lifted my chin and said, "I'm here, Darlene. You won't walk this alone." My missteps would not undo His love, neither the ones I'd already made nor the ones to come.

Jesus tries to reach us at all costs, even unto death.

So never be afraid to simply show up. You might just witness a miracle.

Chapter 10

Sunshine and Lightning

Salem, Missouri

Pregnancy rounded my body, and my tiny frame gave way to life pressing against me from the inside out. And, that's what it did to me too—infused life from the middle of me, flowing outward. I worked as a waitress at the Village Inn restaurant, scratching down orders for customers and waddling back to the kitchen with the requests; until one late night, after many hours of intense labor, our baby boy arrived, lungs crying out in the bright white hospital room. I held him against my chest, feeling his heartbeat find its pace with mine, his face the picture of perfection. That moment told me that even out of my weakness miracles could happen. Joe cried when he held our son—the culmination of our oneness evidenced in our little boy.

But, motherhood didn't always come easy, though loving Joeie did. I prayed for him as he grunted and squirmed in his bassinet. "Jesus, You know his days. Thank you for this gift. Help me to love him like You love me. Wholly and completely."

Joeie continued to cry, hours later, despite all my efforts. Only a small lamp broke up the grey-black of the front room. The wall clock read 2 a.m. Joeie's red face broke my heart, and I hushed him, rubbing his tummy with my warm hand. I'd called Daddy because Joe didn't know about caring for babies and because exhaustion made me think I might collapse. A knock found its way through my baby's cries.

Daddy stepped in and said, "Well, what's wrong, little man?" He reached out and offered a kind smile, took my son, and pulled a warmed hot water bottle from his coat pocket, and placed it across his forearm. Then he laid Joeie, belly first over the bottle, cradling his tiny face in his hand and then began pacing the room, rubbing his small back, and singing softly. He looked over at me where I stood, thinking I might just slump to the floor and sleep like a dog on the carpeted living room floor, and said, "Darlene, go on and get some rest. We'll be alright." I stood there, feeling guilty for leaving my daddy to do my job, but fatigue won the argument inside me.

Tears clogged my throat and I nodded. "Thank you, Daddy." I shuffled back to my bedroom in our tiny house and closed the door, climbing into the bed beside a snoring Joe and pulled a pillow over my head.

I thought of Daddy's kind of love, the gentle, "get some rest" kind of love. *That's true love.* And I fell asleep to the beautiful sound of his feet pacing the living room as he prayed softly, and to the softening cries of my baby boy.

Joe's moods wavered between near-blinding shine and lightening. I wondered who I'd meet at the door after a long day of him working at his dad's logging business. Some days it was sweetness—him pulling me in for a kiss and whispering, "I love your hair. You look beautiful," his smile transforming his face. And others were the yelling kind of days, when life must have pressed down too hard on him, and he'd tear me down with a single sentence. "You're worthless."

Those words, the tearing-down words, fit well into what I already believed to be true—that my own anxieties and failures proved I'd never be useable by God. I struggled just to comfort my little boy. I never lived up to Mom's expectations. And now Joe echoed the ache with a tight, pinching grip and a hiss of disappointment.

Joe leaned on the nearest dryer at the laundromat, staring at his shoes. I'd gotten off my shift at work, and the washing couldn't wait. The hum of the clothes tumbling around and around in the machines lining the wall calmed me. This was one of Joe's dark-mood days, when nothing I said fit with what he wanted.

His brother, Bill, shoved some coins into the slot of a washer in the far corner and pressed start. A hiss of water spray muted the sound of my thoughts. When the washer buzzed that our load was done, I reached in and began pulling out the wet clothes. But then I dropped a massive heap on the ground, and Joe was there to put me in line. He grabbed my upper arm and squeezed the soft skin there so hard I knew it would bruise.

"What the hell are you trying to do?!" His voice cut through the whirring. "Can't you do anything right?"

I mumbled my apology, agreeing with his assessment. I messed everything up. I reached down to clean up my mess, placing the clothing in the basket more carefully this time.

But then Bill walked over, his hands clenched into fists at his side, and he got close enough to my husband to relay his message without making any more of a scene. "Don't you ever lay hands on her again, Joe. Got it?" His eyes simmered with barely-bridled violence.

Joe nodded and snatched a heap of the wet laundry, taking it to the dryer. He slammed the door and stalked over to a chair on the other side of the laundromat where he could glare at me without his brother seeing.

Chapter 11

Lies

St. Louis, Missouri

My belly swelled with new life once again, though my feet walked our new apartment near St. Louis, swollen and achy, far from Salem, and the comfort only Daddy seemed to bring. Joe had needed to find work, and he'd gotten in at the American Can Company because of a connection with my older sister Faye's husband, Al, who also had a job there.

I worked at the mall, trying to help with the expenses of life. When Tamie arrived, the placenta came first, empty and eerily hanging like a grocery sack. But then my baby girl arrived, screaming air into her lungs, and a new wave of love filled my chest. *How can I love them both so much? Thank you, Jesus, for the precious gift of my children. Despite me. Despite my ever-present failings, You did it.*

"What are these bruises, Darlene?"

My brother-in-law, Al, turned Joeie's back toward me, and just above his small bottom was a large purple-blue smudge. I shook my head, pinpricks of grief dotting my lips, my face, down my arms.

"Oh, he fell." The lie put such an instant hatred for myself into my chest it might as well have been a nail in my coffin. I died a little that day because I knew what the colors on his pale skin must be.

Joe and his heavy hand of discipline—with a thick leather belt or his palm on soft flesh—was the cause. It was how his own daddy handled his son's behavior. That, and weeks of punishing silence. But not Joe—his disappointment came out in loud words and the snap of leather on skin. But I might as well have held his hand, bringing the strap down on my three-year-old boy's skin, because I let him do it. Fear kept me from interceding, and fear kept me from voicing my heartbreak. Kept me from protecting my boy.

I turned from Al's probing stare, knowing he must see the word "LIAR" flashing there like a neon sign.

Chapter 12

Hanging over the Canyon

Joeie's Words

St. Louis, Missouri

Sometimes Daddy was as fun as a summer thunderstorm, all splashing and laughing. Sometimes he seemed like he might crack lightening on my head if I didn't do stuff right. It seemed like I couldn't ever be sure whether he'd be glad or mad at me.

I heard his engine rumble outside and I peeked over the windowsill out at him climbing from his car. I watched how he closed the door. *Too hard? Or, just right? Is his face all bunched up or smooth and smiling?* Then I'd run to my room before he snatched open the front door, 'cause I wanted to be sure that the daddy who walked through was the kind who would play nice with me and not swat me with his big fat buckle when I said something stupid. Seemed like I was always doing something stupid. Him being around, as tall as the tallest tree, always made me feel jumbled up inside. *How come I love him so much some days, and others, I wish he'd just leave Mom and Tamie and me alone?*

The door slammed, and I waited. I heard his voice mumbling against Mom's and the tight knot in my stomach loosened up a millimeter.

I peeked my head through the door opening and then tiptoed out. Then I stuck my head around the corner to the living room where they sat and talked.

"Hey there, buddy!" He said, reaching for me. And I knew, today, he was the nice kind of daddy. The kind I wished he'd be every single day.

Daddy put his fists up with the big old round boxing gloves bobbing in front of his face. "You have to jab, like this." He showed me how in the air near my face and I felt the air whoosh by me.

I tried for a while and then he said, "Let's go for real now, son."

He laughed as I jumped around him, like a real pro. I lunged forward and hit his shoulder and he lifted his gloves to shove off my hit. Then he popped me so hard in the face the whole room glittered and blackened, and I fell, the room swallowed up in darkness.

Then a pinprick of white spread out to a circle the size of a baseball until I blinked and looked up. Daddy stood above me grinning like he'd just won. But I didn't think it was too funny. Besides, the only reason I'd been knocked out was 'cause I was four and he was older and bigger.

Tears filled my eyes and I wiped them with the back of my glove.

"I didn't hit you that hard. Quit being a baby."

And I knew not to argue. Daddy didn't like that. Not even when we were playing games.

Sometimes Daddy thought his jokes were funny—only I didn't think so. We went to the Grand Canyon when I was nine, and I ran up and down the sidewalks close to the metal railing until Mom called me back to her side. She reached a warm hand down to me and said, "Stay close, son."

I looked over the side, and it dropped—down, down, down so far I could only see an itty-bitty snake of a river at the bottom, winding its way through the orangey rocks. The picture made my eyes cross and I pressed my face into Mom's side for a second. I wasn't scared. I just didn't like looking for so long.

Daddy picked me up from my waist and lifted me higher and higher, swinging me from side to side, walking closer to the edge by the wobbly metal fencing. "Scared?" He laughed, then jerked his arms forward so my legs dangled like strings outside the only protection I had. I felt like a wiggling bug over the canyon.

"Stop, Joe!" Mom said, her voice sounding like someone had their hands wrapped around her throat. "Please, that's not funny!" I looked over at her dark eyes, her eyebrows pinched all together in a ball.

Daddy just kept laughing. "What if I let go?" Daddy said, his face red, his teeth grinning like it was his most favorite time of our trip.

I hung there as still as I could even though I wanted to scream. Maybe if I moved he'd drop me. I felt like someone had lit a firecracker inside my tummy and I swallowed because I knew crying would only make Daddy laugh more, and maybe he'd let go and maybe I'd fall all the way down to that river and be washed away like a bug on my back. But, maybe that's what he wanted. Maybe he didn't like me at all and he was just telling me what could happen if I didn't mind. Next time, maybe I'd be gone and never come back again.

"Stop!" Mom hollered and reached for me.

Daddy snatched me back inside the fence and growled. "It was only a joke, Darlene."

Chapter 13

Demons Waiting in the Galleys

Salem, Missouri

My third pregnancy was difficult, and I suffered through toxemia. But then my baby girl, Tiffany, was born and the pain echoed and then disappeared. The factory where Joe now worked in Rolla, Missouri, closed its doors, but not before Joe accepted Jesus into his life. He cried like I'd never seen him cry before, so full of regret and thankfulness. After we moved back to Salem, the children and I always attended the church where Daddy pastored. Prior to Joe's life-altering experience, he had stayed home, uninterested. But that changed. The haunted look Joe sometimes had disappeared—releasing him from a prison he had lived in. The change in him jarred me—made me hope for things to be different. *We'll be a family with love and we'll build sweet memories, not the black ones already imprinted on my kids.* And Joe's genuine peace continued, even though his temper still flared from time to time. He still ruled and controlled, expecting obedience on every front, even from me—but a softening occurred too.

He lay beside me in bed one night and whispered into my hair, "I love you so much, Darlene. I'm so grateful for you and I'm so grateful that God loves me no matter what." The "no matter what" hung in the air like a diffusing pollution. Still, it came back later. Because even though I knew Jesus' love knew no end and our mistakes couldn't outreach his Grace, some things couldn't be forgiven by simple human effort. Some things could tear you down, spit you out and leave you to die with vultures circling overhead. And it seemed Joe's demons only waited in the galleys until the perfect time to slink back in.

REFLECTIONS:
HE KNOWS THE STRUGGLE

By this time, it was late in the day, so his disciples came to him. "This is a remote place," they said, "and it's already very late. Send the people away so that they can go to the surrounding countryside and villages and buy themselves something to eat."

—MARK 6:35–36

*T*he disciples told Jesus what was going on, even though He had been with them the whole time. Do you ever remind the maker of heaven and earth about the struggles, as if He doesn't already know? "Jesus, it's late. We're tired. We're hungry. The people are hungry. Can we send them home? PLEASE?"

Then Jesus said, "Give them something to eat."

One disciple said, "How? Don't you see how many people are here? That would cost us eight months' worth of wages! Besides, how are we going to get that much food? Did you forget? We're out in the middle of the desert and there are no stores here for us to get to."

Sound familiar? "Jesus, don't you see what's going on in my life?"

Or maybe, "Jesus, the money is running out. I'm drowning here!"

Or, "Jesus, he's cheating, I just know it. There's no way to fix it."

Or, "My son is becoming an alcoholic and he won't respond to me. I can't do anything to help him."

Jesus hears and He cares, but He also *knows*. He is painfully aware of our struggles—carrying them as a burden on His own back. He sees us in all our brokenness and need. He sees us as if the issues we haul around are materialized and hanging on our shoulders. He tells us again and again, "You don't need to hold that anymore. That's why I'm here. Give those to me." And His capable shoulders can manage it all.

Seeing how my children struggled, feeling the issues mounting and seeing what I knew was only the tip of the iceberg, I felt like I'd drown in the pain of it all, like I'd drown in my own weakness. I wanted God to transform my marriage—to turn it into something beautiful. I wanted to see my kids whole and healthy, childlike smiles replacing the anxiety that hovered. I called out to Him, telling Him all the ways things were falling apart, but the truth was that He already knew.

There is no need to remind Jesus of our sorrows. Instead, offer up your struggles to Him.

Kneel before the King, lay the gargantuan load down at His feet, and petition Him for those needs.

"Jesus, provide."

"Jesus, heal my marriage. Help me know where I am wrong. Help me to let go, if that's your will."

"Jesus, help my son. Let him encounter You so that everything changes. Give him the strength for what's ahead. Give me wisdom on how to help and not enable him."

He'll lean down, press a warm hand to your head and grab the load you left behind to carry it for you. And, He'll walk alongside you as you take steps forward. The problems won't disappear like fog against the sun—but He'll be there, ever patient and loving, smoothing your hair back and hushing the fears. And, beyond the moment of pain, He offers a future and a hope—one that cannot be ripped away by circumstance or abuse or harsh words from an angry husband.

His hope is the eternal kind.

Chapter 14
Spotlight and Praise

Salem, Missouri

Joeie had won contests, even at the age of ten, for his ability to play the bass guitar and sing. And, we began to perform as a family—first just at local churches back home again in Salem, then fanning out and playing more often—sometimes even nine times in a single week—at places dotted across the United States. Joe played guitar and sang with Joeie and me. Joeie was on the bass, with Tiffany on the tambourine, and Tamie playing the drums. That became our full-time living—traveling to local churches and singing about the hope of Jesus. I loved the movement and purpose of our life, and I loved reminding people of God and His faithfulness. For the first time, vision infused me with strength. Being a part of something that could transform an empty life into one with hope filled my chest with a new lightness.

Joe glittered as our charismatic leader, pulling people to himself with his bright white smile. But his eye wandered, and he offered extra compliments to women at the churches where we visited. That was just his way. He'd always made people laugh and feel good about themselves. But, I remembered Trudy and the twisting ache in my stomach when I considered what might have happened on that date, smack-dab in the middle of us being together. And, I wondered if he could be pulled away again by someone new and exciting. He was a man, after all.

Mom changed as a grandmother. She took my babies in as her own, often sending them home from a day with her and Daddy, their arms burdened with gifts—sometimes a new package of undies tucked in the mix. I watched her pull each one up to her, offering a hug and a smile, and I wondered what happened to the woman with few kind words for me and an excessive amount of sadness. But, she even softened towards me. Still, she could tear me down in one sentence. Old habits were hard to break, and she often had thoughts on how I should be raising my kids, rarely pointing out where I did well. I watched her pleasure in my children's funny comments or talents and I realized that, indirect as it was, her pleasure shone on me some too.

Chapter 15

Bumble Bee and Yellow Top

Joeie's Words

On the Road

We had parked our trailer in front of their house in Houston, Texas. The heat snaked above the street and I wiped a hand over my forehead. We all stood around outside talking to the family who'd said we could park there while we did our singing—at their church and at a few others in the area. I eyed the man, a big old guy with hair that looked like a black, flat carpet sitting on the top of his head. Sometimes it seemed like it slipped to the side a little because of the heat.

"Well, we're sure glad to have ya," the man said, his face as red as a cherry Ferrari.

Dad stepped forward, his face wide with a smile, and shook the man's hand. "Thanks for putting up with us!" Then he made introductions, even though we'd met them before. It was what he did every time. "You remember my kids, Joeie, Tamie, and Tiffany. They each play instruments. And, of course, my wife, Darlene."

Again, the man shot out his meaty hand and shook Momma's small one. She smiled and said, "We are so grateful to you."

Just then, the black-haired man's wife stepped out of the house wearing a bumble bee-yellow top, her hair looking as big as a beehive. The hair and the shirt seemed like they'd been put together specially to draw a person in.

"Well if it isn't Lizzy, Lizzy," Dad said, as if she was his best friend. I watched his eyebrows go up and down, and his grin pull up on one side like it always did when a pretty woman was around—kind of like he was hungry for honey. Then, he commented on how her body looked in that yellow outfit.

Momma said, her voice soft and pleading, "Joe, please."

But the man with the toupee laughed, and Lizzy laughed way too loud. I squirmed and looked down at the cracks near my tennis shoes. My face felt as hot as if I'd stood in front of a blazing fire. But it wasn't because of the Houston weather. It was because of Mom standing there like a thrown-out piece of trash, trying to keep her chin up while Dad made eyes at the lady with the way-too-tight shirt. *What's so great about her anyway?* I wanted to punch Dad and punch the man and tell Ms. Lizzy to go back in and change into something more ladylike. I swallowed down the shame, wishing I could drop into a deep dark hole—with everyone but those three fools—and run away.

Dad grunted as he lowered himself to the ground from his height of six feet two inches tall. I arranged the tools on a cloth, so he'd have easy access. Dad counted on me to help with all the duties on the road. When we rolled down the highway, all sorts of problems came up.

The linkage on the bus had broken again. Seemed like that was always happening. "Hand me that wrench," Dad said.

My fingers ran over the tools laid out like soldiers. I knew that he expected me to know the correct size, but just now I couldn't seem to pick right. I snatched one up and placed it in the center of his greasy hand. He twisted on his side, so he could reach the spot underneath that had snapped, and then popped his head up and glared at me, his eyes slits and his lip tight.

"What the hell's wrong with you? This isn't what I asked for. What are you trying to do?!" He hurled the heavy, metal tool at me, and it struck my shin so hard it felt like I had been hit with a bat.

I swallowed and swallowed, the pain howling up my leg. *Don't cry. Don't cry.* I blinked against the tears that came anyway.

Dad tipped his head and scowled. "You're such a wuss." Then he grabbed the larger wrench and got back to work.

Chapter 16
Promising to be Gone

Salem, Missouri

Mom tugged my hand, so we could talk more privately, away from the ever-present eyes of the other parishioners. She'd grown more and more unhealthy over the years, as diabetes and high blood pressure forced daily intake of medication. Mom stood in front of me, arms crossed over her chest, the tight curls she always wore framing her round face.

"When do you go back out on the road?" She stared at me and that old feeling of being a little girl (instead of a grown 27-year-old woman with three kids) rose up like an old corpse. Only, I wasn't so different from that little girl. Even with my own husband I mostly felt small and so very scared.

Somehow, I'd meandered back into a corner, dominated again by another person. I knew well enough from seeing Daddy dealing with Mom, even at her worst, that not all marriages were like mine: a sort of kowtowing to the moods of the brooding leader. But I sought peace. I'd always wanted that. I wanted Mom to be happy with me, for Daddy to smile and laugh and be carefree, and for Joe to quit returning to the dark side of himself, like a mousetrap with a hair-trigger temper. *I'm in danger of being snapped in two.*

I swallowed against the sandpaper in my throat. "We'll be heading out in a week. You know that, Mom." We always came home for the holidays and rested before heading back out on the road in the spring. The schedule had been the same for years now.

"Yes," she said, vinegar entering her voice. "I know that." She stood there for an eternity before saying, "And when will you be back?"

Where were the kids? Upstairs running around? Still in their Sunday School classrooms? I wanted them there for fortification and because maybe the sweetness would re-enter Mom's voice. "In about four months." I knew she loved our singing as a family, especially seeing the children on their instruments. I recalled long-ago days of her tipping her head back, a minuscule smile edging her mouth, eyes closed, listening to us playing in our living room. But I could see that the separation bothered her.

Though it was Daddy and Mom who babysat my kids when I needed help, it was Daddy who sat with me and talked with me about life and motherhood and marriage, and though it was never Mom who expressed that she loved me or longed for my time—in this moment, with her standing as overbearing and intimidating as ever, I saw behind the cloak of aggression to the broken woman.

She stood there as fragile as Depression glass but looking as unmoving as a boulder.

Her eyes snapped like tiny firecrackers and she said, "Well, just so you know, I might not be around by then."

I stayed quiet, unable to speak, then stumbled over my words, begging her to remove the threat that her life would be extinguished before we got back. Still, I remembered back to that day when she sagged like a lifeless doll against the bathroom door, a shotgun in her hand.

I remembered pounding on the door, my hands stinging, crying and screaming for her to come out and not to end her life. Powerlessness numbed my arms and hands.

"Mom, please," I whispered. "Don't say that."

And she turned and walked away. I watched the set of her shoulders as she moved from me. And I wondered if she'd just pull the trigger this time.

A week later, I went with Helen, my longtime friend, to her appointment with the doctor who'd be delivering the baby out of her swollen belly in a matter of days. I sat in the waiting room, Helen fidgeting and trying to get comfortable beside me, when the phone rang. The receptionist picked it up and paused. She looked over at me, "Are you Darlene?"

I sat forward, the plastic seat creaking. "Yes."

"You have a phone call."

Mom. A drum roll began in my chest.

Daddy's voice vibrated in my chest. "I'm sorry to have to tell you this, Darlene. But your mother is gone." He said something about complications from diabetes and blood pressure, and his words wove in and out of me. But I knew better. I knew the real cause of Mom's death. Her doctor had warned me on her last visit.

He'd pulled me aside and said, "She's taking too much of the medications. She can't do that. She's going to die if she keeps on mixing and over-taking them."

And, it seemed to me that Mom had warned me, and because I hadn't listened, she'd exacted her final punishment. She was gone and the ache of loving a person so hard to love deepened. And anger soaked into the cracks she'd put there. *You win, Mom.*

Chapter 17

Don't Stir the Dirt

On the Road, Texas

The dream held me captive. I sat with my back pressed against an enormous tree, the canopy above scattering shadow and light across the forest floor and over me. I could hear him moving, body slithering over dry leaves, long ago shed, now dead and musty. His body moved them in a sort of scraping hush—scales moving around the tree, behind me on my right, then around to my left. Then his face moved into my periphery, tongue flicking, smelling and sensing, making me aware that he saw me and controlled me. *If I stay still, he won't hurt me.*

My heart felt too large to be contained in my chest, the fear swelling there strangling away any scream I had inside. And the snake glided by my feet tucked under my bottom—glided by, his back scattered with shadows too. The light illuminated each scale, the flex of muscle pulling him around the tree again and again, closer and closer until he made a revolution, his one eye nearest me, finding mine. He lifted his face to hiss in my ear, a skittering of fear dancing over my shoulders, down my back. He lifted his face to kiss my cheek. *He's so close.* Panic held me down, pinned my body against the forest floor, pinned my back to the bark.

Don't stir the dirt. Don't move. He'll kill you if you do. Then he disappeared again, his tail the last thing I saw, flicking out of view, his length rounding the base of the tree. And though I couldn't see him, still I heard him and felt him, his presence as real as the tree biting into my back.

Though terror told me to shut up and stay put, another voice lifted me off the forest floor, made me jump to my feet and scream, "Leave me alone in the name of Jesus!" And I ran. I ran as hard as my legs could manage. I saw the arc of light ahead, showing me the way out of the dense overgrowth of pine-green and black. As I neared my escape, people stepped into the woods, passing me, pulled toward the snake and the tree as if by some invisible fishing line. I yelled, "Don't go that way! You don't want to! Don't let that thing imprison you!" And just as I plunged into the light, a searing pain blazed on my heel. I knew the snake had nipped at me but hadn't punctured deep.

And then I knew. *I'm safe. I'm free!*

Chapter 18

Painted House

On the Road

I snatched up my towel and toiletries bag, needing a shower. Tamie looked up from her book, curled in the corner seat on the bus. "Where are you going?"

I noted the anxious look on her face, the scrunched-up eyebrows, the widened eyes. Then she began the rapid blinking that had become her way. Joe looked over and grunted. "Quit your blinking, Tamie!"

"I'm going to take a shower," I said, offering a smile to my girl. Joe's loud demands never alleviated the problem—they seemed to only worsen it.

She stood, grabbing at her things. "I need one too." She looked over at Joe then at me. "Don't leave without me."

I swallowed back a sigh. I needed time alone and it seemed like the bathroom was often the only escape I had. "Of course, I won't leave without you. Go get Tiffany too. We'll all go together."

Soon after, we stepped out on to the campground's dirt-packed path to the women's restroom and showers. I took in a cleaning-out breath, willing the anxiety down. Looking over at Tamie walking beside me, her towel pressed to her chest, I noticed her shoulders had lost their sharp peaks, her face had relaxed, and she blinked like a normal twelve-year-old once again.

Joe pulled the bus into our driveway. We were home for a short visit before heading back out. There would be time for visiting family and for attending to business and, I hoped, for some rest. But, I looked out the front windshield and my house, once white, was now painted a creamy beige.

"Oh, who did that?" I didn't see my dad doing such a thing without asking. Not that I wasn't grateful—the house had needed a fresh coat of paint.

Joe said, "No idea."

But then Susan, our neighbor, walked over from her home—she'd been the one to check in on the house from time to time—and I could see her guilt. "Do you like it?" she asked.

"Oh, you did this?" I didn't know what to say. This woman, one who I suspected had designs on my husband, who Joe seemed to take a special interest in, had painted my entire home.

What are you covering up? What are you making up for?

Joe just grinned and said, "Well, aren't you just the sweetest thing?"

Susan smiled and eyed him before dropping her gaze to the ground and looking at me, her cheeks tinged red.

"I hope you like it, Darlene."

Joe boomed, "Of course she likes it! It looks great."

My stomach felt sour, and I tried to form words, but nothing came out. Just a lame nod before I turned away to begin unpacking the bus.

Chapter 19

Confronting Dad

Joeie's Words

Salem, Missouri

I sat on the sidewalk with my neighbor, Sasha, her hands draped over her knees. She looked over at me, her mouth set in a straight line. "I think it's happening. Your dad and my mom." She looked out over the street, past the houses, to where the trees met the sky.

"Do you know for sure?"

She only said, "Let's just say you should confront him about it. See what he says. How he acts."

Even at 16, there was no romance between my neighbor and I—only a long-standing friendship made of cords knit together in hardship. "I'm scared," I said knowing Sasha would understand.

She nodded and let the sound of the frogs roosting in the creeks nearby speak the sorrow into the darkening sky.

I talked to Dad's back as he tinkered with the bus parked next to the carport, open to the sky. It was nearly time to go back out on tour and I needed to voice my suspicions before I was trapped in a small bus, for hours on end, with no real escape. "Are you sleeping with Susan?"

He turned, a bear caught with his kill. His eyes narrowed. "What did you say, son?"

Before I got the words out, he launched at me, pinned me to the side of the bus, a tool clattering to the ground. "How dare you! Who do you think you are?" He screamed, though his face was inches from mine.

"Is it true then?" I couldn't help but yell back, but my words were muted by tears. "How could you? How could you do that to Mom!"

"Shut up! You need to know your place." He allowed my body to slack away from the side of the bus, then shoved me down and pointed his finger at me. "Shut your mouth. Get out of here. You're a sick pervert to even say such a thing!"

I tasted metal in my mouth. You just answered my question, Dad.

Chapter 20

Blinking and Shadows

Rolla, Missouri

I made the appointment with a specialist in Rolla, and Tamie got into the front passenger seat beside me looking small and scared. I touched her hand. "It'll be okay, sweetheart."

I needed to get to the bottom of it, the blinking. I'd asked her, "Do your eyes hurt?" A shake of her head. "Itch? Maybe it's allergies." Another shake.

Joe had stalked in earlier that morning and bellowed, "Knock it off, Tamie!"

I stood, *"Let's head on out." You aren't helping things!*

Tamie blinked all the more, looking panicked that his words had only increased the rate of her fluttering eyelids.

"Quit or I'll make you quit!"

Jesus, help me. Something's wrong. I feel it.

We took the main road to where the eye specialist had his practice. *Breathe. Breathe. But something's wrong.* I swiped at a stray tear that managed to escape. Hold it together for your daughter. Only, before I knew it, the road turned into a blur in front of me and breathing became harder and harder, like I was inhaling through wool, like my chest was being compressed.

I pulled my vehicle to the side of the road, cars whizzing past on the left, buzzing and then quiet. A flux of power, then quiet. "What's wrong, Mom?" Tamie asked, crying herself. "I'm sorry, Momma."

I pulled my girl to me, her hair smelling like apricots. "You don't need to be sorry about anything, you hear me? I love you. I'll be okay. I just need a minute."

She pulled back, looking at me as if to check to make sure I wouldn't fall apart right there on the highway. Then she just held my hand until my world steadied and I could pull back out onto the long road to the doctor.

Later, the doctor looked at me, his face serious and still. "I can't find anything wrong with your daughter's eyes." He paused, looking down at his clipboard. "I think it's time to consider that Tamie is trying to tell you something else." Shame rolled over me. Pummeled me like a seashell under a wave.

Something is wrong, and you don't even know what it is or how to fix it. What kind of mom are you? And no matter how I asked, Tamie shook her head, eyeing her hands all twisted up in her shirt, blinking like she needed to see past this too. "Nothing's wrong, Momma."

All the way home, the road hummed under the steady, rapid thumping of my heart.

Tamie sought the refuge of her room and I sought mine. The house was so quiet. So empty yet screaming with something I didn't understand. I closed my bedroom door and went to my bed, coaching myself to calm down, to breathe in and out, needing to rest and pray. But then I saw the note, like a death certificate, sitting on my pillow.

My hands shook with the rattling that had begun that morning, jarring my heart against ribs that I felt sure couldn't contain the motion. I lifted the paper and opened it, the sound of the paper crinkling against the quiet.

Darlene, I love God and I love my family, but I don't love you anymore. -Joe

And the room collapsed around me. I set the note down, spread out on the bed, facedown, moaning out the anguish I'd only just barely kept at bay. The culmination of pain heaped on pain. The ceiling seemed to press down and all I could do was moan like a child who no longer knew if she existed anymore. I don't love you anymore. *I don't love you anymore.*

You're not enough for him. You've never been enough.

Vague shadows passed by my periphery. Joeie and Tamie and Tiffany, near the bed, touching me. Only I couldn't climb up. I was at the bottom of a hole that might as well have been all the way at the center of the earth, it felt so deep. A tiny pinprick of light remained. And I cried until my room filled with darkness.

When Joe returned, he barely looked at me. Just resumed life as if my heart hadn't been ripped out and then shoved back in my chest, disconnected from the life source.

We went back on the road. I swallowed against the ever-present pain in my throat, looking out the window as towns whooshed by, greys and blues and browns flashing through me. We had obligations as everyone's favorite traveling family of singers for Jesus. Susan and her family kept up the house while we were out of town, and, even though I had my suspicions about her and about Joe, I pushed them back into a corner.

Make him fall in love with you again. Make him look at you like he once did—like he looks at other women now.

The time blurred together. I tried even harder to look more attractive to Joe, hoping he'd remember what he once saw in me. But, even though we shared a bed and shared our bodies, he always pulled back away, like a shadow finding a deeper darkness. The words he sang to a packed sanctuary about love and the ever-faithful presence of God didn't seem to mean anything to him anymore. They were just part of the act. Part of keeping up appearances.

"Can we go to see a counselor together? Maybe it would help," I said.

He glared at me from his slumped position on the small bus couch. "Maybe you need help, but I don't."

My world spiraled out of control, the foundation jarring, cracking, splitting. *Jesus, help me. What do I do? How do I save my marriage? How do I protect my children?*

God spoke to me in the quiet of the night, our bus parked in some stranger's driveway, Joe snoring beside me. The beast was at rest. Joe seemed so consumed by darkness—the hope he once had now indistinguishable. God quieted the voices that told me this was all my fault, that I caused the disquiet in my husband.

And my Lord showed me things, lasting things, like stops on a long road leading to an orange-yellow horizon. A vision of people, Africans, a sea of dark faces and a love so consuming it made me struggle for a breath. *What are you saying, God?*

I didn't understand, but I did know one thing. He was telling me I had a future and a hope, come what may.

Chapter 21

Masks

Joeie's Words

On the Road

It was my job to help with the full equipment set up. Roll out the cables just so. Tape them down. Set up the mics and instruments. Make everything look perfect. I squinted a bit as I unwrapped another coil of cable in the church sanctuary, stringing it along so that it was the least noticeable from the audience's point of view. It was always about that. What was seen. What was heard by strangers. Not anything about the truth—about what our lives as a traveling family singing group was really like in private. *Smile. Perform flawlessly. Make Dad look good.*

As I had done many times before, I pulled out the tape from the roll, the high-pitched sound grating on my nerves. We used the tape to keep everything attached to the ground, seamless, so nobody tripped over cables, and nobody in the congregation had to endure the visual hardship of too many wires muddying their view. Mom worked quietly helping Tamie get her drums set up, and Dad walked in and out with more instruments from the bus, dropping them in a heap before turning on his heel and going back out.

I used my teeth to tear off a piece of tape and then laid it flat along the cable, smoothing it down with my fingertips. Then I moved further down the line. My mind wandered to the last place we'd been, singing about Jesus even as I wanted to escape. *I'm in a cage. I need out.* None of it felt right anymore, and anger had built so tight in me I thought I might snap, and then I'd be just like Dad—like a live, severed wire in a puddle of water.

As if on cue, Dad yelled, "What the hell do you think you're doing, Joeie?" My stomach lurched, and my heart felt like a rag in a dryer, end over end. I looked over my shoulder at where Dad stood, and at Mom, whose eyes changed to those of a rabbit's, beat into a corner. "How many times have I told you to do it this way? And for some reason you can't get it through your idiotic skull to do it right!" He pointed to the offending strip of tape, and I wracked my brain to figure out what I'd done wrong this time.

Dad ripped up an entire line of tape, undoing in one second what I'd taken a half hour to set up. He balled it up like an old sweater and tossed it at me, then walked over and tugged me up by my collar, whipping his fist back. I closed my eyes, waiting for impact. His face looked like it might explode, it was so red. And the veins in his neck bulged, cables unfettered. Spit landed on my face as he screamed, "I'm sick to death of repeating myself to you!"

I hated him in that moment. Hated the small blood vessels around his brown eyes. Hated the hand that held me in a vise grip. Hated the way he looked at other women and how he would look at Mom like he would kill her if she dared talk back. Hated how he treated Tamie like an acquaintance he just tolerated. But mostly, I hated his hypocrisy.

"Joe, calm down, please," Mom said, her voice sounding like a beggar-woman's.

With a final shove, he let go and left the room, the cloud of his darkness hovering like poisonous gas.

Mom tried to comfort me, but I couldn't hear her because the pastor of the church had entered the sanctuary with his unaware grin and pressed suit and grateful praises and said, "I'd love to take a photo of your beautiful family, if you don't mind."

Mom looked over at me, grief as real as if it were woven into a cloak pressing down her shoulders. She nodded and said, "Sure, Pastor. Let me just run and get Joe."

Soon Dad returned, the mask back in place, smiling like he'd won some stupid contest, and I wondered how he managed it. How he could go from so dark and hateful to everyone's favorite performer.

We all clustered together as a family to pose for the picture, Mom holding Tiffany, Tamie standing just in front of me, and Dad on my side. He slid his hand up to the muscle just beside my shoulder blade and pinched so hard it brought tears to my eyes. I blinked them back, trying to look happy. I knew it would leave a mark, but that was nothing new. He leaned his mouth close to my ear, his breath hot and his whispered words only loud enough to be heard by me, "If you don't smile, I'll kill you."

So, I did. I played my part, though the rest of me felt like I'd been shattered to pieces.

Soon the people who'd come to hear the perfect family play their perfect songs filed in, excitement in their voices like those of children at a party. Mom offered all she could: a look that told me she understood, that she felt the same, that her heart was broken too, that she saw my bitterness, and that she loved me anyway.

Dad called the audience to attention with a smooth, "Thank you all so much for coming out. We are so blessed to be here." And then he began his rote introductions. It all blurred and faded out until I got roped back in with his words, "And my son, Joeie, the most talented guitar player I know." I hated myself for the feeling of pride that surged at his words. *You know it's all just a part of the act. He's not proud of you.*

I swallowed back the acid that filled my throat. *Just do the songs. Just get through it and it will be over and then you can leave.* So, I did. I moved my fingers over the strings, knowing where they belonged instinctively, loving the music despite the liar who led us.

I watched Mom's face. So sad. Eyes drooping down in the corners. Tears brimming like water over the edge of a dam wall. But it was too much. All of it. The fake smiles from Dad. The false compliments that only really served to elevate him—make him look like the holy family man with a perfect family and perfect kids and perfect love for Jesus.

"I'm leaving," I said. The world fell in crumbles. Massive boulders once held in place by mortar now gave way, threatening to bury me. Threatening to pin me in—to turn me into him.

I finally said, "I can't do it anymore."

Mom reached to me, a hand on my elbow, so gentle. Never hurting. Always loving. But that didn't change the facts.

"You can't leave now. We're in L.A. Where will you go?"

"I can't do it anymore. I won't let him treat me like this anymore." A shake riddled through me, and I swallowed the ache in my throat. "If he ever lays a hand on me again, one of us is going to die," I said through a tight jaw. I meant the threat. It was alive in me, the anger. It was clawing to be let out. *Fight it. Don't be like him. Don't become like him.*

Mom nodded, the tears falling now like rain across Missouri, across the land we'd traveled as a family, across the entire world. She pulled me in, so much shorter than me. She whispered, "Please don't leave, son." Then she pulled back, so I could see her face.

Her eyes, the color of molasses, wouldn't let me go. Her love held more sway than all Dad's controlling—the pinning down, the beating down.

I'm old enough now, but that doesn't mean anything. I can't go. What about Mom? What about Tamie and Tiffany? No. I wouldn't leave. I'd stay because of them.

Then she pressed back in and cried into my shoulder. "I can't protect you anymore."

Her tears broke free more boulders, and I thought I'd be crushed.

Mom, who always tried to diffuse Dad's moods and rages. Who said, "It's gonna be okay. Why don't you kids go on out and play?" And then turned to face Dad, taking the brunt, while we wandered out and away from the firestorm. She pulled back now, smoothed my hair, telling me she loved me in that small action.

"I'm afraid he's gonna kill you," I confessed.

She didn't let go but only said, "I'll be okay, son. Please don't worry about me." Her warm hand pressed into mine, trying to say all was well. But I knew better.

Chapter 22

Prayers on the Bus

On the Road

Every morning, early, before my family began to move about the bus, getting ready for a day of homeschool, performances or a day of driving over borders, I prayed. The private hallway, tucked at the end of the bus, closed off from the seats, closed, too, to the small bunks and bathroom nestled on each side—that place, became my refuge with Jesus.

Sometimes I thought of Daddy, sending his words to the heavens on our behalf, and I did the same. Quietly, so as not to disturb the kids or Joe, I spoke. I told God about the hurt, the worry, about the failures and fears. And He listened, an attentive father, and comforted me. I knew even the broken things, the places torn to shreds, could be reached if I offered them up to Jesus. I spoke of my children, asking God to remind them that, despite their father's actions, He never left, never failed, never gave up, and was always faithful.

The sun rose into the sky, and Tiffany, just seven years old, crawled down from her bunk bed, out through the door into the hallway.

"Praying, Mom?"

"Yes," I said.

"Can I pray with you next time?"

"Oh, but you're always sleeping so good when I get up." I buried my fingers in her wild bed-hair.

"Still, I want you to wake me up, okay?" She laid her small hands on both sides of my face and landed her sweet rosebud lips on my mouth.

"Alright."

The next morning, I opened the small door that led to her bunk. I gently shook her shoulder, and she sat up, bleary-eyed and warm. "Praying time?"

I nodded and whispered, "Praying time."

She stayed tucked under her covers, reaching her hand to mine, and I held it, beginning to pray softly enough to not wake the rest of the family in their cubbies. But, minutes in, her grip relaxed, and a minuscule buzzing sound started up. I smiled at my girl, her tiny hand in mine, and thanked God for the gifts He'd given me.

Chapter 23

Her Eyes Are Wounds

Joeie's Words

Heading Home

The bus drove over endless roads, it seemed like. The quiet inside the vehicle made me feel like punching something. Dad wouldn't speak, just eyed the asphalt in front of him like it was his Bible, packed with answers to whatever he chewed over.

Mom looked out the window, her pretty brown hair pulled in a loose ponytail, little strands of it dancing in the wind coming through the cracked window, an almost invisible stream of tears making a river on her cheek. She wiped it away with her shoulder, so maybe we wouldn't notice, but it didn't help. The grief in the bus was alive.

We were going home early. Dad had said so, announced it with no explanation. The shift had happened after an earlier trip he and Mom had taken to attend the funeral of a man we'd met on our travels. Dad had eyed the widow, Laura, and flirted like he'd done with everyone else, but this was different. A decision had been made.

Back home, Dad dropped us off, parking our bus next to my grandparents' house.

He pulled me aside to talk, and the only thing he said was, "I'm leaving."

I resisted the urge to say that he'd already done that. That I hated him and wished he'd left a long time ago.

"Is this for someone else?" I asked, "Are you leaving us for someone else?"

"No," he said, looking the picture of sorrow, his eyebrows pinched and tears filling his eyes. "Why would you say that?"

The words clogged in my throat like vomit. *Because you've been sleeping with our neighbor, and now, most likely, you're doing the same with Laura!*

He shook his head and walked into the house.

Tiffany looked up at him, so small and innocent. "Where are you going, Daddy?"

He kneeled down and said, "I'm going to get a job. I won't be back for a while." Genuine sadness seemed to take over then, and he held Tiffany for a time before letting go, standing up then, hugging Tamie then grabbing at his belongings, taking all that he cared about. Then he left.

In the bedroom, Mom cried and cried. She cried so hard she couldn't catch a breath. Her small body curled in a ball on her rumpled blankets, and her hands covered her head. The brokenness throbbed in the space. A brokenness so deep I knew it would tear her in two if I didn't do something.

The ambulance arrived. As they lifted her onto the gurney, she just kept on crying. I wondered if the crying would ever stop, if we'd survive this. If Mom would die and fly off to heaven and leave us here to wonder what to do next.

She lay on her side, her eyes revealing the open wound of her heart, her arms curled in front of her. I wondered how blood could keep pumping through such sad, delicate flesh.

The doctor said, his voice steady and firm, "She's had a mini-stroke most likely brought on by all the grief. If you don't give her a reason to live, she's going to die of a broken heart." I looked over at her face, half covered by her hands, and swallowed back the tears.

Are we reason enough, Mom? And I reached out and touched her hair, and her whole body seemed to relax and calm. Peace. *For now.*

Chapter 24

Stuck and Drowning

Salem Memorial Hospital, Salem, Missouri

I stared down at my hands. They shook, and I folded them together, a metallic taste in my mouth. "Darlene, look at me," my family doctor said.

My time in the hospital room was a blur of faces, prayers whispered over me, Daddy's warm hand on my head, the kids' tentative, worried expressions.

Still, I felt dazed—broken. I found out that Joe had returned to the Carolinas, returned to Laura. The pastor of that church called saying, "I thought you should know."

We'd sung, Joe and I, at Laura's husband's funeral. I'd prayed for her. Easter was just a week away and images of my girls in matching dresses and Joeie in a suit and tie danced in front of me.

The struggle to keep thinking, thinking, thinking exhausted me—thinking about what went wrong, about what I could have done to prevent his infidelity, about what she had that I didn't, about how I'd put one foot in front of the other and survive the days ahead as a single mom now.

How do I help the children understand all this when I can't? How can I help them move on when I'm stuck and drowning?

"Darlene?"

He eyed me and waited until he could tell I had engaged, until he saw that I wasn't somewhere else again.

"Darlene, listen to me. If you don't pull yourself together, I'll have no choice but to have you sent to the state hospital in Farmington. And you'll lose them, Darlene. Do you hear me? You'll lose your children." He paused, the wrinkles between his eyebrows more pronounced. "Well, hell, Darlene, you can just lay there and die, or you can raise those kids! Or Joe can."

I watched Dr. Carnett's mouth move, his words taking shape and growing teeth. *You'll lose your children.* I thought of Joeie's face, his full-of-heart, fiercely protective eyes. I thought of Tamie's motherly kindness to me, of her independence and courage. I remembered Tiffany's little hand in mine, saying, "Praying, Mom?" And I knew I would not give up. They were my gift. They were my joy, and I wouldn't let them be taken.

REFLECTIONS:
LYING BY THE POOL

I am reminded of the man in the Gospel of St John, chapter 5, lying by the pool for 31 years—just waiting for someone to come and lift him into the cool waters. Like him, I did my best with what I had—with what I knew and with the strength in me. I loved God and wanted to follow the path He led me on. But, I came to a place at 33 years of age with three beautiful children where I had to choose between life or death.

Jesus asked the man lying by the pool the same question my doctor asked me, "Do you want to be made whole, or do you want to slip away and miss this awesome journey of life and the good plans I have for you?" I, like the lame man, felt I had no one to help me out of my situation. Life as my kids and I had known it was over. But God showed me in an instant that my life was not intended for me—it was intended for His Glory.

His Glory was to be revealed in how my children saw His story in me.

I bit the inside of my cheeks, deciding that Joe's choices need not defeat me. They didn't need to define me.

I belong to the Most High God! My children, too. I am loved and treasured. He is always present. He is always faithful, and He won't leave me alone. I'm choosing to live, Jesus, but I need You to hold me as I do it. I can barely walk.

The following Sunday, after I had made a life-changing decision that would change me from a place of weakness to a place of strength, a local pastor came and offered me communion. And as I drank that juice and ate the bread, I knew the stone had been rolled away in my life and that I would walk in the resurrection power that was inside of me.

The choice I made was monumental. Oh, the faithfulness of God! God heard my every cry and saw every tear shed, and He made a promise.

"Let's bury this and you'll see my power. Explosive, whole and joyful life will come from what was dead."

Chapter 25

Pain Doesn't Have to Reign

Salem, Missouri

"Daddy, I don't know what to do. He wants a divorce, but I know it's wrong. I told him I wouldn't give it to him."

Daddy took his glasses off and rubbed out the smudges with his white button-down shirt. He waited long enough that I knew he was thinking, probably praying for wisdom.

"You're right. Wedding vows are until death do us part. But, Darlene," he said, his face showing grief for me, for my suffering. "You've had a death in your marriage." His words hummed, resonating in me.

I considered his wisdom. My daddy, the only man in my life whom I totally trusted and who I knew loved God with all his heart, had told me it was okay to let my marriage go.

The phone rang, grating on my nerves that felt like wounds barely covered in a paper-thin layer of new skin. I pressed the receiver to my ear, the long coil of phone line spiraling from the kitchen to the living room where I walked.

"Darlene, I wanted to tell you that I'll be coming back to Missouri to get the rest of my things. I'll be bringing the papers."

Quiet. I had nothing to say. All my words dried up and skittered off like leaves down a closed-off road.

"Did you hear me?"

"Yes. When?"

"I'll be there tomorrow."

I shifted from one foot to the other, the plastic of the phone irritating my cheek. "Please just don't bring Laura with you. Please don't do that to me, to the kids."

"I would never do that," he whispered, sounding more grieved than I thought him capable.

He did come, wearing a gold chain around his neck like a drug dealer or something. I signed his ugly papers at his lawyer's office and stood there like a statue. He packed up his things and took the bus, because he called the shots and what would I do with it anyway? Then, he drove away. I watched the lights until our home for the last seven years looked like two tiny red eyes at the end of an empty street.

I found out from his mother that Joe's bus had broken down on his way back to the Carolinas, outside of St. Louis, Missouri. He arranged with his brother, who was a mechanic, to go help. His mom told me all of this with a sliver of hope in her eyes, like I could get him to return now by just showing up on the side of the road. With very little money myself, money given to me by generous churches who'd heard about how Joe had left, I knew I couldn't do much. But still, I stuffed a small wad of cash in my purse and hopped in Joeie's vehicle, a beaten-up token from his dad, driving the long highway until I spotted the bus at a truck stop. I pulled into a nearby parking place and walked toward the bus. I swallowed down the fear that threatened to make me get back in my car and pretend I had never been there.

Joe spotted me and stalked toward me. "What the hell are you doing here, Darlene?"

I reached a hand into my purse and pulled out the cash. "I just wanted to help, to give you a little money. You said you had no money," I finished lamely.

He glared at me like I'd set the whole thing up, that I'd made the bus break down so that then he'd need me again. "I don't want your money. Go! Get the hell out of here!"

A quaking took over my limbs, but, somehow, I managed to lift my chin, turn away from my husband whose face looked ugly to me now and walk back to the car. I got in, gripping the steering wheel, the tears I'd refused to give in to coming now. Tears blurred the gray road ahead of me, but I managed to drive the hours back home, praying all the way.

"Jesus, I don't understand! I know he doesn't want me. But why can't I at least help him?" I spoke to God about the hurt, let it tumble out in the small cab of the car. "Jesus help me!"

Later that evening, my brother-in-law came by and said, "Darlene, are you okay?" He paused. "He got so angry because Laura was in the bus." He was quiet for a minute before adding, "I just thought you should know. It wasn't your fault."

The one thing I'd asked of Joe, he ignored. He must have brought Laura to Salem because why else would she be in the bus just hours outside of town? And something in me let go of him then. Knowing that I couldn't trust him with even that one request caused me to open my tight grip to the sky, unclench my fist and let the breeze carry off the scraps I had held onto with a death grip. *I'm letting him go, Jesus.*

Easter Sunday. A new day. A day that said pain doesn't have to reign. New life can break out of any tomb—even one covered by a stone so huge it took four soldiers to move it. And so, with feet that hurt with every step, I moved forward. Counting the blessings: my Tiffany's arms wrapped around my neck, her cheek pressed softly against mine; Tamie's posture opening up, lifting her chin, changing visibly, like a sunflower after a long time away from the sun; Joeie's protective hand in mine, showing me that he loved me and was proud of me.

Jesus, you are my strength and my salvation, my ever-present help in time of need.

Crickets stroked their legs against the night quiet, and the phone screeched against the calm. I snatched up the phone, pressing it to my ear.

"Darlene," Joe breathed.

"Joe."

"I just needed to hear your voice."

What? My voice? When you've clearly chosen to fall asleep with someone else's voice saying good night?

Tamie stepped into the kitchen, so still, looking at me, wrapping her arms around her tummy then quietly exiting, hunching her shoulders.

"I miss you," Joe said.

"What do you want?"

"I was just thinking about that one time when ..." And I tuned him out as he spun through our history as if he still owned it—even though the divorce would be final in less than a week.

Before we said goodbye, I told him, "Joe, I'm done. The kids and I will be okay." I wouldn't be his sounding board for his guilt or regret. He wanted two worlds—one that required true love and one that expected nothing.

And he seemed to accept that we wouldn't be talking and reminiscing about the good-ole-days that never were that good. He seemed to know that pulling on me, like a small plastic figure on the end of a long string, my body scraping cement, wouldn't work.

Then I hung up, quieting his voice.

But not completely.

"Mom?" Tamie said as we sat together on my bed afterward. "You aren't going to let him come back, are you?" She tucked her feet under her bottom and pulled the throw blanket around her body, looking like my little girl swaddled in white.

Part of me wanted to scream that I still needed him, but I told that girl inside me to shut up. "No, Tamie. I won't. We won't be treated that way anymore. We all deserve better." Saying the words out loud, words that had begun germinating only days before, gave them life. The truth fortified me for what would come next. Single mom or not, my children were my gift, my responsibility, and letting them be toyed with and tormented wasn't fair.

And, for the first time in a long time, I felt just a little bit strong.

PART TWO

Chapter 26

Saying "I Do" Again

Salem, Missouri

No, in all these things we are more than conquerors through him who loved us. For I am convinced that neither death nor life, neither angels nor demons, neither the present nor the future, nor any powers, neither height nor depth, nor anything else in all creation, will be able to separate us from the love of God that is in Christ Jesus our Lord.

—Romans 8:37-39

Pastor Mike, Joe's mom's pastor, told me about a friend of his who'd gone through something just like me. "Darlene, I can't pretend to know what you're going through, but I have this friend who pretty much had the same thing happen. His wife left him, and he got custody of his kids. He's a pastor over in Farmington. He maybe could be a support for you. His name is Darryl Rhodes."

A thought skittered through my mind. *That's the same place Dr. Carnett spoke to me about—the place with the state hospital where he nearly had to send me.*

"Oh, that's funny. I know him."

"Well, you know a lot of pastors."

"Yes, but we met something like 18 years ago. Back at a church camp. We wrote letters for a while."

"Hmm ... Seems like a pretty neat coincidence, don't you think?"

I picked up the phone, feeling a tingling in my lips, in my fingertips. Talking about all this pain seemed like a terrible idea—it was so raw. But I felt I needed to connect with another human being who'd been through something similar, so I wouldn't convince myself, again, that it was all my fault. I needed to be understood. I wanted to know why everything fell apart for Darryl. Maybe it would make more sense to me then, too.

I called the church office in the evening, thinking I could leave a message and talk later. "You've reached Calvary Temple; may I help you?" The woman's voice sounded so sweet and eager I hated to hang up on her.

"Yes, my name is Darlene, used to be Darlene Hassell. I was given Pastor Darryl's name because ..." *What? Because I was left by my husband just like he was left by his wife?* The words sounded ridiculous. "We knew each other a long time ago and ... Pastor Mike gave me his name saying it might be a good idea to call." *Well, that sounded just awful!* I cringed, thinking the woman surely thought I was a lost and pathetic woman.

"Do you mind holding on for a second?"

I breathed deeply and waited. In a minute, a deep voice hammered into my spinning thoughts. "Darlene?"

I stuttered for a solid year before saying, "Yes, this is Darlene. From church camp," the idiot in me continued. "Pastor Mike told me just a little about your divorce and suggested I call you. He thought maybe it would be good for me to talk to you." I finished with, "Because my husband left, and we were in a traveling singing group, a ministry." I just decided to quit talking because I figured I'd done enough damage.

"Well, I'd be happy to get together and talk. Where do you live now?"

"Salem."

"How about I drive your way soon, and we can catch up?"

The knot in my chest eased back a little. It felt less like a pity meeting or even a counseling session. It seemed more like two old friends sharing.

I can do this.

Darryl had changed a lot since we were both in middle school. He'd sprouted up and broadened too. He offered a beaming grin when he pulled into the parking lot and got out of his car.

"Darlene! Gosh, it's been a long time." He pulled me into a bear hug and then released. "You look just the same."

I couldn't help but smile at his enthusiasm. I felt small next to his imposing figure. "You don't," I said.

"Well, you know, I've grown a tad." Again, with his winning smile.

We sat down at a corner table, and he began to share. "You know, when my wife left, I felt like my world fell apart. I didn't see it coming. Did you?"

I nodded. "I didn't admit it to myself, but I saw the signs beforehand. And I tried so hard to fix it." I looked down at my hands, feeling naked in front of this near-stranger but, somehow, at ease. "But I couldn't. He didn't want it to be fixed. He just wanted out."

He leaned in, folding his hands. "Yah, definitely has to be a mutual thing. Did you get custody of the kids?"

"Yes. He didn't want anything but the bus." My cheeks grew hot ... knowing that I hadn't been good enough, at least not in Joe's eyes. I'd only just begun to see the difference between Joe's opinion of me and all my shortcomings, and God's generous view of my heart.

As we talked, I realized he had fought for his kids—tears burned in my eyes. He actually cared more about them than his own comfort. I had never seen that with Joe. No, it had been all about him. All about his pleasure and glory and pedestal.

Darryl appraised me for a second before saying, "Darlene, I know this hurts more than most anything. But there is hope. The pain won't be so sharp forever."

We talked for hours, and time slipped by. And when we said our farewells, I knew something had lifted, one layer of many to come, I was still very aware of the pain, but it had softened just a little—like water over a jagged rock, making the edges round and smooth.

Darryl stayed overnight at Pastor Mike's house. Around midmorning, he called on his way back home. "I'd really like to see you again," he said, his voice outlined with vulnerability but also something else. Something that yelled out, "I am not a walking dead. I'm alive and won't back down from a fight. I know who I am." And though that pulled on my chest, like the magnetic force of his strength, I couldn't move forward. Not yet.

"I'm just not ready for a relationship, Darryl. It's not fair to you or me to pretend I am." *Broken things don't fit together well anyway. Not without a lot of glue and duct tape.*

His deep, kind voice said, "I understand but ... you wouldn't want to have a cup of coffee before I leave, would you?"

Of course, I would. You make me feel like I won't always be this frail. But I'm scared to death. "I guess that wouldn't hurt anything, would it?"

"Not at all," he said, and I could tell by his voice that he was smiling.

Joeie hunched over his guitar in the living room, concentrating on his fingers moving over the strings like the instrument belonged there, an extension of himself. Tiffany and Tamie sat in the chairs, and Darryl played his guitar while Joeie and I sang. The lamplight glowed in the space and, despite there being another man in my home interacting with my kids, whom I now felt fiercely protective of in a life-or-death sort of way, a calm warmed my chest.

I didn't understand what was happening. Despite the boundary lines I'd drawn with Darryl, he didn't give up on our friendship. Though the girls, especially, had pushed back when Darryl began spending more time with us, they softened—they seemed to understand that he wasn't self-seeking, that he cared and that he loved God. Our connection was easy and comfortable, and nothing like things had been with Joe, tiptoeing around topics or being afraid of insulting his pride. Darryl extended a lifeline to me, drawing me back to shore out of a shark-infested sea.

Even Daddy liked him and said with a knowing glimmer in his brown eyes, "He's a good man, Darlene." Something he'd never said of Joe. And the kids seemed at ease around him. None of the landmine interactions they'd experienced daily with their dad.

Darryl carried the peace of God in his heart—just like Daddy did. I found myself comparing the two more and more. The similarities easing back the concern that rose up now and then about ever loving another man in the way a wife loves a husband.

And then one Sunday afternoon at his house, standing in the great room he said, "Will you become my wife?"

Fear clawed up telling me to run, telling me that getting trapped again in a controlling relationship would kill me. "Are you talking about marriage?" His words made no sense. I wasn't ready. "When?"

"Soon." He lifted my hands with his fingertips. "It's not good for us to date for long. Me being a pastor. You know all about the fishbowl."

"Darryl, I'm so vulnerable right now and so scared." The clock ticked on the wall, insistent, pressing into me.

"I know, Darlene. And I don't want to take advantage of that. But I believe with all my heart that this is God's will for us."

I had my doubts. Had I ever thought, deep in my chest, that Joe was the one God had for me? A vision of standing in his living room with Daddy saying to him, "I didn't come here to tell you to marry my daughter." I considered that maybe that *hadn't* been God's will then. But without that marriage, I wouldn't have Tamie and Tiffany. How could I tell the difference? I saw how God brought beauty and blessing even out of my mistakes, but His will ... that wasn't something I claimed to know.

Darryl rubbed a thumb over my hand, and his eyes shone with tears. And he waited for my answer.

When I talked to Daddy about my future and my precious children, he placed a hand on my shoulder and said, "I believe Darryl is a godsend. He loves you, Darlene."

Even on the morning of the wedding, I questioned, "Am I doing the right thing?"

And like a deer with the lights shining in her eyes, I said, "I do," feeling it was the right decision despite my terror.

Darryl pulled up to the store, and said, "You go ahead inside, and I'll just go park the car." When I didn't move, he looked me in the eyes and added, "Meet you in a few, okay?" The car hummed under me, rattling me, jarring loose the tightly tucked away fear that never disappeared, always reminded me of how small I was.

My heart felt compressed, and the air grew so thin. *He's leaving me. He knows now what he's gotten into and wants out. He'll never come back!* Images filtered in. Belongings being snatched up and piled into the bus. Divorce papers with my signature-line empty. A pen handed to me. Joe waiting for me to give my consent for him to walk away. Bus lights glowing against the dusk.

Darryl pressed his lips to mine then drew back enough to say, "I'll come back. I promise." I searched his eyes, so close now, soft brown orbs that said, "Believe me. I'm not like him." And I chose. I chose to take him at his word, feeling the calm returning to my numbed limbs.

And Jesus whispered the real truth. People will fail us, but He said, "I will never leave you nor forsake you."

Chapter 27

Spirit Wounds

St. Louis, Missouri

Look at me. I'm a pastor's wife. I always imagined myself being a part of the ministry in that way. Now the old dream tapped on my shoulder, asking me to remember where I'd come from—that my hopes had been fulfilled in this way. But inadequacy nipped at my heels, reminding me of the little girl who was afraid of her own shadow, afraid of harsh words from Mom, afraid to stand up too tall, the girl who dropped out of high school and never went back.

"Back in a sec, Babe." Darryl pressed his hand to my shoulder then was gone. I sank lower in my seat in the large meeting room, feeling the sudden loss of heat, the loss of his imposing presence keeping me upright. He made me strong, and, without him, I didn't know how to be the woman everyone expected me to be. The enormous space full of people threatened to swallow me up. I felt like a drone bee in an enormous hive, beating my wings to keep from dying. The room seemed to press in on me, like the walls were on sliders, pressing on me, on my chest. My heart hammered and made it hard to take in enough air. *Jesus, I need you. You are my strength. I'm here because of you, so that's the reason I don't have to be afraid.*

I counseled myself until the panic subsided, and my heart quieted. *I can do this because of you, God.*

How can I be and do all the right things? I preferred a quiet room, surrounded by silence, praying and listening, to the in-the-spotlight role I had to play now. I'm nothing, Jesus. And I'm scared to death. Still, two worlds tugged against each other: the one where I felt as small as a speck in the middle of the ocean, where fear ruled me, and the other where I stepped into something brand new, where I spoke about the healing blood of Jesus.

The dream that had remained vivid over the years of the snake and the fear and the powerlessness, pressed into my mind, like a note telling me to pay attention. I remembered the feeling of the forest floor. I remembered the terror. I remembered the hiss and the kisses and the temptation to stay put, to not stir up trouble. *If you'll only just stay in your place, you'll be okay.*

But I was sick of survival. I was sick of rails narrowing until I felt I couldn't move. I was fed up with old words playing in my mind, telling me to shut up, sit down and quit causing trouble.

I wanted to stand and scream to my past, to my self-imposed prison, "Get away from me in the name of Jesus!" And run. Run into the freedom Jesus had been waiting all along to give me.

Tulsa, Oklahoma

"For you, Lord, are good, and ready to forgive, and abundant in mercy." The pain wouldn't let up. Billy Jo Dougherty continued the closing of the service after Jack Hayford's stirring preaching. I fidgeted in my chair, unable to settle down. Of course, he knew nothing of my torment as he spoke. I wanted to cover my ears and sing loud enough that his voice would go away, along with Hayford's message still echoing through my chest.

Billy Jo pointed right at me. "The lady sitting up about the 10th row, will you come down here? I want to pray for you." I scooched down in my seat, tugging the grey blazer down as if I could use it to cover myself enough not to be seen. He repeated the words, and I tried to comprehend.

Someone tapped me from behind. "I think he's talking to you."

I looked up, touched my chest and mouthed, "Me?"

"Yes, and is that your husband?" Billy Jo said into the mic.

And again, I nodded.

"Bring him with you."

We wove our way to the front, and he spoke directly to us. "You are not second-class Christians, and God's plans have not changed for your lives just because the enemy tried to steal them. God's anointing is on you. Go back to your hotel room and forgive every person who has hurt you. Let them go and let the hurts of the past go."

In our room at the hotel, I let the ache out. I believed that God was asking me to forgive Mom, to release her words and her actions and her displeasure, to let them out of the box I'd kept them in for so long. In that space, I'd shoved my bitterness, thinking I hadn't held on to it. But so often the old hurt echoed, like screams in a canyon, pain throbbing against stone walls I'd built.

"Lord, help me." I spoke out my sadness to the quiet, knowing He heard. "Help me forgive her." I knew the box held tight against my chest would keep me from stepping out and being able to tell about the all-consuming, hold-nothing-back love of our Jesus—the kind of love that allowed hands to be nailed into harsh wood and still said, "Forgive them."

And the Lord showed me my mom, a woman wounded by her own old shadows, perpetuated, most likely, because she had her box of woes too. I saw Mom as a broken person, riddled with pain, trying to be whole when she'd only been glued together, never really healed.

And seeing her that way allowed me to let go and remember her as a fellow child of God, struggling, as I so often did, with the lies I told myself.

"I forgive you, Mom. And I love you."

After that I let the other old hurts tumble out. Joe and his spirit-wounds to me and to my children. I forgave my cousin who had stolen a piece of my childhood and devoured it. And, somehow, God restored what he'd taken.

I let the hold of those wounds chink off, like a hunk of mountain that had been weighing me down with fear and shame. *Jesus, take it all. I forgive. I am letting go now.*

Chapter 28

True Love and True Peace

Tiffany's Words

Farmington, Missouri

At nine, I felt afraid inside all the time. Afraid to go to sleep. Afraid to look at Daddy during our visits and hear the lies he told about loving us more than anything else. Afraid to find out he didn't love me at all. Darryl was kind and took care of us, but all the changes bounced inside me. I felt jumbled and off-kilter, like I'd slip and fall any minute.

The last time Tamie and I visited Daddy, a terrible thing happened. We stood on the front porch watching Daddy back out his big old 18-wheeler truck. The long vehicle inched backward, and, just then, a man in a car rounded the curve going so, so fast, not paying any attention to the road. His car sliced into the trailer on the back of the truck. Tamie and I just stood there on the front step of the house, watching the whole thing happen, like it was in slow motion. The man died in an instant, the force of the accident taking his head off. Blood sprayed the front window, and the sound of metal squealing and my own screaming filled my ears.

From that moment, the terror wouldn't go away. I couldn't escape it. It had lived there before, but the accident let the fear out of the box.

Daddy Darryl stepped into my room and sat on the side of my bed, his weight tipping it to the side a little. "Goodnight, Tiffany. Sweet dreams."

Tears burned my throat because I knew they wouldn't be sweet. Nighttime gave my brain time to quit pretending about my fear. Nighttime gave it time to grow and smother me.

"You alright?" He watched me and waited.

I couldn't hold back the words and the sobbing, "I'm so afraid!" I poured out the truth of my constant anxiety. "I don't even want to go to sleep!" Then the dreams would come, images of cars and blood and Daddy's smile.

Daddy Darryl and Mama had come in enough times in the middle of the night, woken by my screams. "Tiffany, I know it seems like this will never get better, but it will. But you have to let God have it. Don't hold it inside." He stopped for a second and said, "Let's pray again."

I nodded, wanting God to make it all better.

He pressed a warm hand over mine. "Dear Jesus. Would you comfort your child? Would you take away the fear and replace it with courage? Please comfort her and remind her that you are near and that you will never leave her. I pray she knows that you'll fight this battle. I pray she'll feel your peace."

And something did change in me. I understood true love and true, deep down calm, like the way a lake looks when all the fish are asleep.

I slept soundly that night. I didn't dream one bit.

Chapter 29

Dreams Reaching
the Horizon

Pastor's Conference, Texas

The crowd stirred as Daisy Osborn took the stage, placing one high-heeled foot in front of the other, then standing behind the podium, looking out over the throng of people hungry for a refreshing. I'd heard all about her, and the ministry she led that called people to tell all about the love and hope of Jesus to people all over the world.

Daisy wrapped her fingers over the edge of the podium and seemed to look straight at me as she began to tell about how all of us are equal in God's eyes, all of us have the same place of honor and value in His kingdom, all of us have been called and anointed and strengthened and loved and equipped to change the world—no matter the gender, no matter the color of skin, no matter the weakness we perceive, no matter the education or lack thereof.

And as she spun her words across the enormous room, I saw it. I stood, seeing the same dark-skinned women and children filling the space all the way to the horizon, countless faces looking towards me. I spoke and taught and shared my story.

REFLECTIONS:
"GO AND SEE WHAT
YOU CAN FIND."

"How many loaves do you have?" he asked. "Go and see."
When they found out, they said, "Five—and two fish."

—MARK 6:38

The disciples wandered around that hillside, most likely thinking, "What's the point? We will never find enough for all of these people." They must have thought that Jesus' admonition "go and see" was naïve. "Alright, Jesus. But this is a waste of time."

So, they looked and found a boy sitting amongst the throng with his lunch, most likely packed by his mama, in a basket by his bare feet. With a sigh, I imagine, one disciple asked the boy if he'd be willing to share. I wonder what the boy thought? Was he childlike in his inability to see the absurdity, so he simply nodded and grinned, clueless that it was nowhere near enough? Was he confused but relented anyway?

In my story, I stepped into an overwhelming buzz of people, and all I had was me—weak and most of the time scared to death. But I offered it up to a loving Father, and He smiled and said, "Darlene, I'm not scared by the little bit you offered. I don't fit inside the meager offering anyway. I'm going to take it and transform it. Just watch."

"Go see what you can find," He said.

He doesn't need "enough." He just needs you to be willing to step out on that hillside and trust Him to do the rest.

Chapter 30

Brown Wings Against a Blue Sky

Eldoret, Kenya

Pastor Julius accompanied us to the orphanages where we brought supplies and toys, later preaching in the village nearby.

Darryl stepped up to the rickety platform made with scraps of wood, discarded and now reused. I followed him and sat to the side, looking out over the crowd of men and women packed into a grassy area, the sun beating down without taking a break. He spoke to the men and women of the community about the hope and love of Jesus as kids played and laughed. The brightly colored fabrics the ladies wore made the place appear to be a patchwork quilt that lived and breathed and swayed. Many included swaddled babies pressed against breasts, tied on with swatches of purple. Several little boys used sticks to bat around a rusty tin can, scraping along the red-brown dirt. And love for these people swelled inside me, consuming the space in my chest where my heart tried to keep up with the intensity of the feeling.

Darryl spoke the words to the song I would sing next, so the interpreters could explain their meaning before we began. "Oh, Lord my God, when I in awesome wonder, consider all the worlds Thy hands have made ..." And the lyrics, beautifully echoed in Swahili, wrapped around me, told my own story back to me: from a place of captivity to a place of restoration all because of Him! "*Bwana Mungu wangu, wakati mimi ni ajabu, fikiria ulimwengu wote, Mikono yako imefanya ...*"

Earlier that day, I'd sat with a woman, fever producing dots of perspiration over her forehead, and prayed, my white skin stark against her brown. I'd held a young lady's hand whose sorrows I didn't truly grasp but somehow felt connected to, and together we cried and called on Jesus for newness. And I'd pressed the fuzzy head of an infant to my chest where he slept and sighed as the smell of the mess in his cloth diaper reminded me of his illness.

This was only the beginning. And hope rose in me like a sandgrouse—flapping dull wings up from its place of camouflage on the dry ground, up into the sky, seen and offset by the vibrant blue.

Chapter 31

A Dream Coming to Pass

Nakuru, Kenya

The rain fell on the crowd of over 3,000 registered women in Nakuru. Children glistened and wove in and out of the mass of beautiful dark-faced females. The ladies, wrapped in multicolored fabrics, leaned back on their hands or leaned forward with faces propped in palms, listening intently as I preached about Jesus and the hope and power He offers, about the deep love He extends.

Afterward, we worshipped together, lifting rich voices to God, smiles so white against shades of brown skin, dancing to the rhythmic drum slapped by palms anxious to be heard.

Thank you for loving these women so much, Jesus! Thank you that I get to tell them all about You!

The last evening of the meeting, a young Kenyan man said to my husband, "Not since Daisy Osborne has anyone come and spoken the heart of God to our women with so much love, power and authority as they've experienced in this meeting through the Word spoken through your wife."

When my husband shared with me what the man had said, I remembered that meeting so long ago when the words of Daisy Osborne stirred in my chest, and I saw a beautiful patchwork of color and African faces—a vision of what was to come.

Lord, You are so good and faithful! You took a girl who was scared to death and made her bold enough to share truth with thousands! Only You, Jesus. Only You!

Chapter 32

Heart and Healing

Farmington, Missouri

Back home, I continued to help at the church and helped with the school housed there. I thought back over the last conference in Kenya and smiled.

Only You, Jesus.

I was sitting at the desk in my office and working through the program open on my computer, when my heart fluttered, like an erratic beating of wings inside my ribs, then a pause and another flutter. The room began to swim and tilt, and I yelled out toward the front office, "I need help!" I knew enough to plant my head between my knees, praying the world would come back into focus, for sharp lines to replace the wavy ones. Darryl ran in and placed his hand on my shoulder.

"What is it, Darlene? Are you okay?" Fear edged his voice like the dark outline on a pastel drawing.

"I don't know." We waited, and Darryl prayed and slowly the feeling passed.

Later that evening, we drove to St. Louis and celebrated our oldest granddaughter's twelfth birthday, but I knew that something was not right in my body. The strange feelings abated for a few days but returned with greater and greater vengeance. So, we made an appointment with my doctor to make sure everything was okay, and he referred me to a heart specialist.

The diagnosis came in two, enormous, terrifying words: ventricular tachycardia. "Simplified, it is characterized by irregular electrical pulses, causing your heart to race or beat irregularly." The doctor paused. "This can cause your heart to struggle because it is beating erratically and not allowing time for your ventricles to fill with blood, to pump that to your body, before beating again."

I was sent to a heart specialist in Festus who tried to slow the tachycardia down via medication with no success. I was then sent to an electrophysiologist who did an ablation to stop the erratic heartbeats. After five hours of trying to get the heartbeats under control, the doctor told my husband that he was unsuccessful, and he wanted to send me to Barnes Hospital in St. Louis to his teacher, Dr. Lindsey, an electrophysiologist.

Dr. Lindsey rubbed a hand over his chin. I watched his face, hoping for a glimmer of good news. I'd been through an avalanche of new tests and was tired but still hopeful that God had plans for me yet. "Since your ablation didn't work and because of the place that needs to be ablated is too close to the coronary artery, our only other surgery option at this time is open heart surgery. But I have to be honest, your chance of surviving that is not good, due to the potential of bleeding out. So, I think we should begin drug therapies that may help to regulate the irregular beats."

So, we began the medications, hoping for success.

Four months after my first visit with Dr. Lindsey, I was staying overnight with Joeie while Darryl was on a leadership trip to Kenya and Uganda. I stayed behind and was helping with my grandson, Corey—Joeie's boy. We were headed to the mall to pick up his tux for our daughter's wedding the following weekend, after Darryl would be home.

I pulled the car onto the road, taking a deep breath. Since my diagnosis, I felt my body slowing and struggling. Some days, I just rested in bed, not feeling well enough to do everyday life. Many days I felt glued down, unable to carry myself and function like a normal person. The small highway that connected Joeie's neighborhood with the busy side of town stretched in front of me. But the lines began to blur and blend, weaving in and out of one another.

I saw the orange of construction cones ahead. Orange, grey, white zigzagging.

"Are you okay, Mamaw?" I heard the words, but I couldn't respond. I knew I just needed to get over to the side of the road. I didn't want my boy getting hurt. *Just get to the side.*

A thump, thump, thump and the yell from Corey pulled me to, and I managed to exit into a parking lot in front of a strip mall and a Baskin Robbins. The car tilted in the front to the right, and I knew that the tire was punctured, at the very least. Corey punched in his daddy's cell phone number and told him what happened—said something about the car and about me speaking funny and acting funny. Then he handed the cell to me, taking the keys from the ignition and tucking them in his pocket. I pressed the phone to my ear as Joeie kept talking and talking and asking questions over and over, and I just wanted to lay down and sleep, but he wouldn't let me. And then he was there, and Corey was picked up too, and the street blurred and blurred by until we finally arrived at the hospital.

Later, they told me I'd had a stroke due to a clot at the stem of my brain. They also discovered I had a hole in my heart, probably there since birth, which had nothing to do with the ventricular tachycardia. Darryl found out from across the Atlantic about my stroke and that his mother had passed away but was unable to get home until more than a week later *Lord, I trust you. I trust you.*

I got out of the hospital with a warning from the neurologist. "I would rather you miss your daughter's wedding and live to see your grandchildren grow up." But I didn't want to live in fear. I wanted to live the life in front of me. So, I met Darryl at the airport and pulled him to me, planting a kiss on his lips, and I went to my mother-in-law's funeral, holding Darryl's hand and crying with him. I watched my husband perform at our daughter's wedding, grinning as he spoke blessing over their marriage.

And the next day was Easter. I knew it was a promise that no matter the outcome of my health, God's resurrection power resided in me, right in the middle of my heart.

By the end of the year, I had a cardio-seal placed over the hole in my heart. And the following year, I had Lap Nissan surgery, which involved wrapping a portion of my stomach around the lower esophageal sphincter.

The years that filtered by were marked by more and more episodes, and my medicine was increased to the maximum of what I was allowed to take. According to Dr. Lindsey, open heart surgery or attempting another ablation offered only a mere one-in-a-hundred-chance of success.

So, we waited, and I wondered if everything we did in Kenya and the other places we'd traveled and ministered would be shut down. I wondered if my road was coming to an end on this earth.

In spite of the struggles with health issues, God gave me great grace and favor. Darryl and I still traveled and preached. I still pastored alongside my husband at our home church, and I continued with everyday life. I regularly read healing scriptures and declared that, "I shall live and not die. And I will declare the wonderful works of God!"

When people asked me, concern edging their eyes, "How are you, really?"

I would reply honestly, "All is well." God-confidence filled me. I thought of the little Shunamite woman of the Bible who, confident in the promises she'd received, even when her son died, trusted. And he was raised from death.

Many Sundays, I would get up to get dressed and have to lay back on the bed. Darryl would tell me "Honey, it's okay if you stay home today." My reply was always the same, "Today could be my day for a miracle!"

Every time I walked into God's House and attended church, He would always strengthen me. And I savored my time of worship in His house.

Chapter 33

Speaking to the Beautiful Masses

Armenia and The Republic of Georgia, 2002

Still, we pressed forward, trusting God to allow me to do what he ordained for me in the time he allowed. Darryl arranged a preaching team to go to Armenia and then to the Republic of Georgia with its history of Soviet control, remnants still clinging to the space. He asked the conference host in Armenia if I would be allowed to speak on the leadership team as a team member. Our host in Armenia had responded, "No, I think we cannot do this. A woman will not be allowed to speak."

On the second day of that conference, one of our ministry team members, Pastor Steve, became very ill and unable to minister. Already shorthanded and now down to just my husband and one other man, Darryl spoke again to our host who'd set the week's activities. He explained about the other pastor being sick. He asked about his wife stepping into his shoes, despite hers being so much smaller on the outside.

Our host, being courteous to Darryl's request went to Bishop Rubik to pass on the information, and I was granted permission to speak. After I preached that first session, God orchestrated an open invitation not only to continue to speak on the leadership team but to also conduct ladies' conferences in Armenia.

Bishop Rubik's endorsement was, "You can speak in any of my churches at any time."

After the Armenian conference, we crossed the border into the Republic of Georgia. The green landscape spoke to me, a glistening river keeping stride with our vehicle. Something new growing in the midst of all the beautiful old.

Our hosts for this conference had already approved me to be part of the leadership team, even though this would be a first for them to have a woman preach in their services.

We stepped into the decrepit building, lit only by a few sad bulbs hanging from the high ceiling by long electrical cords, barely illuminating mere feet with their dull glow. The damp space smelled like oppression, built by the USSR, a survivor of the cold war—a reminder to not speak the name of Jesus, to not hope for more.

But soon the place was packed with bodies longing for transformation, the women seated on old benches on one side, the men on the other.

Though I'd preached in the past, at our church back home and in other countries for women, this felt different. This was preaching to men and women at a leadership conference! This was a wall decimated. This was an opportunity with far-reaching aftermath.

Excitement and intimidation took turns with my heart. *God, only You could have opened this door. Thank you for this opportunity. I would never have believed it possible!*

And so, my voice found its way across the clog of people, each word gaining in volume and courage.

John, an older member of our team, later found me, his demeanor full of suspicion and concern. I'd spoken several times now, and he seemed to question the wisdom in that decision. "Make sure the gentlemen don't think you're preaching to them." He squinted and waited, the wrinkles around his mouth deepening in the center. I knew he wasn't happy with the arrangement of me regularly preaching to the crowd.

The trembling I'd kept at bay rumbled in my stomach. "Thank you for your wisdom," I said.

He grunted and turned and walked away.

Before the end of that trip, I couldn't even fit a toothbrush in my mouth, the stress had tightened my jaw so much. Still, I loved the opportunity I'd received. I decided all I could do was preach God's Word—to tell the truth. After that, Bishop Oleg said I could speak at all future conferences and, before long, Pastor John had dubbed me, "His favorite woman preacher." Yes, walls had been blown clean away.

Darryl squeezed my hand and then smiled like he was on the inside track of an inside joke. "See you later," he said, smiling, "The ladies have plans for you." He raised his eyebrows then climbed into a vehicle with several other conference team members and drove away. Even though I watched until his van disappeared in the chaos of the Georgian street, I wasn't afraid. It felt like an adventure—gone was my usual anxiety.

Ciuri, the Bishop's wife, our lady host and I got into a van with a driver and our host's two daughters and pulled out into the dark street. I understood only that she was taking me to some sort of meeting to talk. Ciuri, bobbed her head as if hoping I'd approve, her eyes glittering with mischief.

I only smiled and nodded, since no translator had joined us in the car. But we had gone only a few blocks when the van stalled. There was a lot of loud talk and arrangements made that I didn't understand. My husband was eating dinner goodness-knows-where in the busy city of Tbilisi, and I was on the side of a road in a broken-down van with no way to communicate, but I wasn't riddled with fear. I giggled a little, amazed by the realization. The next thing I knew, a taxi pulled up, and I was ushered into the front seat and the two young daughters of our host climbed into the backseat. The taxi driver was given very detailed instructions and off we went, with Ciuri and the host just waving from their place by the broken-down van.

Our taxi driver yanked the wheel and pulled out into the tangle of traffic, no clear direction to the madness, no rules or order of any kind. He drove, weaving in and out of vehicles and people and bicycles in the cool of the night. Beyond my window blurred a city that seemed medieval-ancient against stark Soviet-drab, like the two worlds had been placed inside a snow globe and shaken up. We passed the Mtkvari River, its green-brown snaking by the shades of blue and cream Georgian-style then Byzantine buildings. As we drove, I remembered the warnings we'd received earlier, that the Russian Mafia owned the taxis in town. The admonition flashed in my mind like the red-hot numbers on the taxi's dash stating the fare—but I ignored it. Darkness had bled the daylight away, and the buildings looked paler and ghostlier than they had in the Tbilisi sunlight. We wove through the city, passing familiar landmarks once, then again. I decided we were going in circles but, again, I wasn't afraid. I looked over my shoulder at the young girls in the back seat, and they only smiled and placed a hand on my shoulder from time to time. *Look at me, fraidy-cat turned adventurer!*

More than an hour later, we were deposited in front of Ciuri's shop, a small room filled with a couch and coffee table. We shuffled in, and Ciuri greeted us, all smiles and kisses on our cheeks. I wondered how she got there but, clearly, our taxi had taken the long way. She waved a hand to a couch with a coffee table in front of it and said, "Sit."

I sank into the furniture and looked around just as the lights went out. I listened as Ciuri's voice and her daughter's voice rose and fell in the blackened space, then total silence. I waited and waited until a match was struck and broke the darkness. Ciuri lit the candle in her hand and placed it on the table in front of me. But nobody sat down with me. Ciuri and her daughter just kept going in and out of a doorway. And then Ciuri's husband, Bishop Oleg, arrived with our hosts and one of our translators, and they directed us into the room from which Ciuri kept shuttling in and out. And there sat a table covered in cakes and fruits and khachapuri, a delicious cheese bread. Candles lit the colorful display, casting warm flickering light on the feast.

"Sit, please," Ciuri said, her bright smile bringing one to my face, too. I realized that I had been seated in a place of honor, the lavish décor and spread of colorful treats all part of some larger message.

The Bishop said, his hands folded in front of him on the table, "Will you be willing to have a ladies' conference next time you visit?" He waited for the translators to do their work, and then it dawned on me. This feast, the stalling in the taxi, the place of honor at the table, were all for me.

My face warmed, feeling so astounded it took me a minute to respond.

Tears filled my eyes, the room swimming in liquid, and I swallowed down the lump in my throat. I nodded and pressed a hand to my chest and said, "Yes, I would be honored."

And so, the next year, I began leading women's conferences for hundreds of Georgian women. And I knew it could have only happened because of Jesus. Because of His strength.

"In John, chapter five, it tells the story of a crippled man who'd lost all hope." I looked out into the dimly lit, cavernous room, trying to make eye contact. A man stood behind a small table, managing the sound. The translator echoed my words, causing me to pause after each phrase. "This man had been sitting on his mat for so many years and couldn't ever get down into the healing waters of the pool of Bethesda. He couldn't crawl fast enough and consistently fell behind the others who could walk."

I paused and looked out at the crowd seated in the chairs, only illuminated by the two bulbs hanging from the ceiling. They remained as still as the damp air inside the room. "But Jesus saw him there and only said, 'Pick up your mat and walk.'" I picked up the blanket I'd tied up and brought from my hotel room as a prop.

"We all have a mat of sorts that we stay stuck on, tied down to. That mat represents your past, whatever situation has caused you to feel impotent, alone, powerless, afraid, depressed. God doesn't want you to stay in that situation. Do you realize that Jesus has paid the price, so you don't have to stay there?"

The movement of the sound controller caught my eye. He pressed his face into his hands and began to weep.

"You may think, I'll always be poor or ugly or weak or crippled or alone. But God sees you. He hears you crying, and He is calling you to get up and walk out your purpose. It's up to you to get up and take hold of that purpose."

Chapter 34

Last Days and New Life

The Nursing Home, 2004

I stepped into the entrance of the nursing home and found Daddy in his usual place. He'd been rolled down to the front room, other people from the facility seated around him as he preached about Jesus' redeeming love. I smiled watching him there, noting the attention the other residents offered, faces alight with hope.

At 96, he hadn't slowed down much. He would have been home with Myrtle, the woman he married years after Mama died, if not for needing rehabilitation after a surgery. He saw me standing there and offered a grin that lined his face with soft wrinkles—joy lines from years of finding his peace with God and knowing his life had value because of belonging to Him.

But the surgery had taken its toll, and, just when we thought Daddy was on the mend and ready to resume "normal life," he got a staph infection. The attack left his body weak, his vibrant brown eyes only dulled a little. In his room, he lay on the bed, his brows twisted in pain. We prayed for him, and Daddy lifted his hand, bony and frail, to his God, praising even in this. Then a measure of relief followed, and he sagged against his pillow. In those last days, Daddy always made me laugh. Anyone who visited saw his peace in going to be with the Lord. He told me about a dream and said, "I came into this wide-open space, it was so big. and people were coming to me, smiling. And I heard them saying, 'There's Luther,' and I could feel the joy." I believe Daddy got a glimpse of his future home.

One night, I curled up against him in his hospital bed, my head pressed to his chest, hearing his heart thump its slow, steady beat. I fell asleep there, peace swirling like incense in the room. When I woke, there was only quiet. My daddy, who had left early each morning to go to the church to pray for his family, who had held me and cried with me when my marriage fell apart, who was a steady grandfather and great-grandfather to my children and grandchildren, went home to be with his Jesus that day.

"I love you, Daddy. And I'll see you there."

At his memorial service, I spoke to a packed room, but I was really talking to my dad. "Daddy, I want to thank you for the inheritance you left to me and my children. Thank you for teaching me the ways of God. The little girl that followed you around, holding your hand, learned a lot about the God-life. I watched as you laid hands on the sick, cast out evil spirits, and taught the word of God to God's people. I was in training, Daddy. I well remember waking up to your prayers or hearing the kitchen door close as you slipped out to the church in the early hours. You taught me how to pray and the importance of praying unceasingly. Even as I visited with you in the nursing home, as we talked, you'd take my hand

and say, "Let's pray." I loved the way you always started off with "Dear Lord" because He was Lord to you.

"You have taught me to never be ashamed of the gospel of Jesus Christ and to not forget that my mission in this life is to fulfill His will, not mine. You've taught me to be honest, to pay my bills and, oh yes, you've taught me how frail we humans can be."

"Thank you for being faithful to the end. You never quit, never stopped dreaming, and never lost hope. You always wanted to go preach just one more time. Your endurance has taught me the faithfulness of God. Thank you, Daddy, for the inheritance you are leaving to me and my children and to my children's children. I will be eternally grateful that you have walked, not just talked, the God kind of life."

Chapter 35

Setbacks and Fresh Heartbreak

Tamie pulled her car into the grocery parking lot, lingering for a moment. "Mom?" she said, looking over her shoulder at me, still gripping the steering wheel, the car humming in idle.

"What is it, sweetie?" I held my purse on my lap, looking over at my baby, a grown woman who made me proud.

But my strong daughter looked uncertain, fragile now. "Do you know if Dad was messing with me?" Her eyes reminded me of an animal backed into a corner. *Is she asking me if I knew, or if it happened at all?*

A whoosh of tingling pain traveled from my face, down my arms and my stomach began a nauseating turn. I couldn't speak. A vision of my little girl, blinking and blinking, and the doctor saying, "Maybe she's trying to tell you something, Darlene," swam and poked against my chest. Tamie snatching up her towel whenever I went to the shower while we were camped at an RV site and insisting on being my shadow. All the pieces made sense. *I missed it! How could I have missed it? Jesus, help me.*

I shook my head and whispered, "No. Please believe me, the thought never crossed my mind." I reached out and covered her hand with my own. My heart felt as heavy as the moon. I could barely get the words out, my throat squeezed so tight and, despite trying to be strong, the tears wouldn't stay in. "I'm so sorry..."

Tamie only nodded and said, "Okay. I don't want to talk about it again, but I just needed to know."

Later, alone, I sobbed in the shower, the water not hot enough to make me feel clean. *I failed her. I missed her silent cries!* I scrubbed at my skin, then later, wrapped my hair in a towel and curled up in my bed.

And Jesus came and ministered to me. "Darlene, this is not your burden to carry. Give it to me. I'm the only one who can heal those places." But it was hard to relinquish the things I felt I'd been called to do—being a mother and protecting my children.

So, I offered the broken pieces back to Him again. I handed them over, though I tried often to snatch them back, huddling over them in pain, as if curling over an injury. But God kept reminding me that He loved me, that He loved my children, Tamie and Tiffany and Joeie, all grown and all loving and all following after Jesus now.

My Lord told me the truth—that no matter what, His love cannot be stolen away, even by something like this.

In the depth of my sorrow, He reminded me: nothing can separate you from My love.

REFLECTIONS:
BROKEN THINGS MULTIPLY

Then Jesus directed them to have all the people sit down in groups on the green grass. So, they sat down in groups of hundreds and fifties. Taking the five loaves and the two fish and looking up to heaven, he gave thanks and broke the loaves. Then he gave them to his disciples to distribute to the people. He also divided the two fish among them all. They all ate and were satisfied, and the disciples picked up twelve basketfuls of broken pieces of bread and fish. The number of the men who had eaten was five thousand.

—MARK 6:39-44

little boy's lunch. Definitely not enough. But still, Jesus lifted the bread made with grain ground by hand, basic and not fancy, and He broke it. And when He did, a miracle happened. The pieces did not reflect the initial offering. The amount, even after everyone had eaten their fill, far surpassed the amount they'd begun with.

A long time later, Jesus would do the same as a representation of Himself, telling His disciples, yet again, that He would allow Himself to be broken, like bread, and then healing and redemption and wholeness would be the outcome for countless mankind. I was broken by many of my life's circumstances. I felt at times like my heart had been shattered on a hard ground, pulled apart. But His loving hands pointed out the beauty in the brokenness, because it all reflected back to His miraculous ability to turn "not enough" into more than enough, with leftovers to boot.

Chapter 36
A Perfectly Normal Heart

Farmington, Missouri

I had made a decision, and I talked with Darryl. Years had passed since Dr. Lindsey had told me about the one-in-a-hundred-chance procedure, and maybe now a more modern ablation procedure made the odds better. And I was tired of just surviving. I refused to live in fear of the unknown.

Besides, I figured a one-in-a-hundred-chance to live was pretty good since I had God on my side. Peace filtered through me like water sinking into the spaces in the sand.

"Are you sure, Darlene?" Darryl watched me as if trying to soak in strength.

"I'm sure," I said.

Darryl and I had danced in our living room that morning to "Look at Us" by Vince Gill, my husband's tears wetting my hair. We said what we needed to say should today's procedure end my life. We kissed and talked. And then, we got into the car, the sky dark as ink, and drove to St. Louis.

The nurses prepped me for surgery, and I lay there praying, asking God to give me strength, come what may.

Later, when the anesthesia wore off and light poked holes into my deep sleep, the doctor stood before me shaking his head, hands folded in front of his body clothed in scrubs, hair hidden by a medical cap.

"Darlene, all I can say is that you've gotten your miracle." He smiled and shrugged. "I went in and tried and tried to agitate the area we've been struggling to get calmed down for eight years now, and it wouldn't do it. It acted like a perfectly normal heart." Then he left the room and repeated the great news to Darryl.

When Darryl, my children, grandchildren and close friends came in to see me, they all commented on the same thing—how different I looked, how healthy and alive.

A few weeks later, I returned for a follow-up visit and, after checking me again, Dr. Lindsey said, "All I can tell you is that you don't need me anymore."

Jesus, thank you. I love you. You are the miracle worker, and I can't wait to see what's next!

Chapter 37

Ending the Cycle

Joeie's Words

Nashville, Tennessee

The pain took me to my knees, and I let myself cry for the little boy who didn't have the dad he needed. I let go of the anger toward him, surrendering it from my place on the ground. I sobbed, needing to let go of the knot of bitterness that had grown calloused—a painful tearing away of hardened tissue—to get back to the heart God gave me.

Later, I picked up my cell phone and texted him. "Dad, I just wanted to say that I forgive you. For everything you've ever done. I forgive you for all of it."

He knew what "all of it" meant, but still he responded with, "I don't see that there needs to be any forgiveness on either side, but okay."

His response didn't surprise me, and it wasn't what I wanted, but I wouldn't go back. *I've released him. It's done.* Unforgiveness had taken more than it had given—and was a cruel master.

Gratitude defined me now—the childhood I'd lived made me stronger, made me sure of who I did and didn't want to be.

As a husband and a dad now, the magnitude of my roles was not lost on me. I knew that words and actions could break a heart or build it up.

I determined to show the love my wife and kids deserved. I decided to be stronger and real, avoiding the temptation to pretend to be better than I am—to make everyone cater to making me look good.

I decided to end the cycle Dad had begun. Come what may, truth would be my measuring stick.

Chapter 38
Walking Free

Republic of Georgia

We sat around in a park after we had finished a conference in the city of Kutaisi. Despite loving the fellowship with our friends, fatigue settled on me like an overly hot blanket, and I sighed. Bela, a young girl who was just a little girl when we first started coming to Georgia, began to tell us where different people around us were from—Russia, Armenia, Azerbaijan, Turkey. She commented with a smile, "It's easy to tell whether a person is from Russia or the Ukraine or America."

"How can you tell an American from any other person?" I asked, noticing that most of the people passing by were Caucasian.

She straightened her body and lifted her chin. "Americans walk with their heads held up." The others around the circle nodded in agreement.

"You mean, we're arrogant?" I hoped we didn't represent that attitude in our demeanor. Darryl and I, as well as the other team members we took with us, wanted to always exhibit humility and kindness. We wanted to show how level the ground is in God's kingdom.

Bela, who was now a beautiful young woman and had attended many of our conferences only shook her head, her eyebrows lifted high. "No, not this. Americans walk with their heads held up." She smiled at me and squinted, small wrinkles forming around her eyes, then she rose to her feet and demonstrated how Americans carried themselves.

"Americans walk like they are free." As I reflected on what she said, I remembered back to those previous years and I could now see how free the women of Georgia had become and how this young woman, and many others, were living testimonies to what God could do in a life, no matter where they lived or came from! No matter the brokenness, too.

Ciuri leaned her shoulder against mine as we spoke, a translator carrying our messages back and forth.

"After you go, we take your words to the villages nearby."

I turned to her, watching her face, so open with honesty and love for Jesus.

"We take your messages to many, many people. This way it keeps going, not just in Tbilisi but outside too."

I imagined the far-reaching message of God's love and hope and purpose, spreading like a tipped over ink bottle to all of Georgia and the people beyond. I smiled, closed my eyes and told my Jesus, "I love you. Thank you. You did it."

The Storyteller

by Morgan Harper Nichols[1]

On a Sunday evening
I'm looking back over all the years
and where I've been
Looking at old photographs
I'm remembering you were right there
and you have been ever since
With every page that turns, I see your faithfulness
Oh, the mountain where I climbed
The valley where I fell
You were there all along
That's the story I'll tell
You brought the pieces together
Made me this storyteller
Now I know it is well, it is well
That's the story I'll tell
There were some nights, that felt like
They would last forever
But You kept me breathing
You were with me right then
And all that you have done for me
I could never hold it in
So, here's me telling this story
Over and over again

---

[1] Morgan Harper Nichols, *The Storyteller* (Franklin, Tennessee: Gotee Records, 1994).

Author Reflections:
His Story

God has performed countless miracles in my life. He took a scared-to-death girl and transformed her into a woman sure of her calling, speaking to thousands! He healed that girl's heart in so many ways, too. I learned I could trust Him with my broken pieces.

But, don't live for the miracles. The power isn't found there. The power is found in the Miracle Worker. New hardships will come. New fears and issues will seep in. But I don't need to fear those. I can look at the future with hope. If I'm living for the miracle, my focus is in the wrong place—on the wrong thing. I'll grow weary when the hard parts stretch too long.

No. Best to look to the Miracle Worker.

He stands out on the hillside, smiling and saying, "I can do amazing things with *not enough*. Just watch." And, He takes the broken pieces and transforms them into overflowing baskets, more than can even be eaten by 5,000.

And, also, He beckons from the middle of a storm, standing there so calm and strong and sure, offering His steady hand when I'm sinking—when I'm sure I'll die this time. He's no different in the calm than in the storm. He is the Lord Most High, though He kneels low to truly see us, lift our chins, dry our tears and settle the score.

It isn't the miracle we need to rely on. It is the Miracle Worker. And His eyes are full of kindness.

You see, I've found that God can use broken things.

I've found that He can multiply them.

I've seen, firsthand, how He can take the scraps and feed thousands, including me in that number.

I've seen the Miracle Worker, and His love and His strength and His generosity are enough for us all. From never-ending to never-ending.

Write Your Story

On April 17th, 1990, at 12:35 p.m., I made the decision to choose joy. I encourage you to look to the Miracle Worker, let Him infuse you with strength. Make a decision to remember who you are, no matter the circumstances, no matter the mess—you are an adored child of God made in His image. You are not a mistake. You are not too far gone. You are not "a product of the system." You are His. Walk in His truth and His love and choose joy!

....

Life is God's Gift to You

Date: _____

I, _____, make a quality choice to be happy in an unhappy world.

Despite people and their attitudes, I have determined and settled with God's help, I shall take His suggestion and choose life according to Deuteronomy 30:19 and Joshua 24:15.

I realize my last "freedom" in life is to determine my attitude in any given situation.

I don't like some of the situations caused by other people. But my choice is to let the Greater One rule, not them. Proverbs 23:7 says, "As he thinketh in his heart so is he."

Happiness is found in holiness. It's a choice of attitude over circumstances. I, today, make an absolute commitment to Christ and to the will of my Father. I want His hand to crush my carnal nature, so I'll be transformed into the image of Christ! I don't want new wine in old bottles anymore. I want the carnal nature "crushed"; the inner poison removed, so complete healing and a NEW BEGINNING can start in my life!

....

About the Author

Darlene has experienced miracles firsthand. She often says that God took her "not enough" and made it more than enough, evidenced in her international speaking ministry to women, her outreach to orphans, and in her co-pastoring with her husband at their local church.

Through her international speaking ministry *Women Around the World*, Darlene uses her story and His Story to bring hope and restoration to those who feel powerless. She has spoken this message to the far reaches of the world, including Kenya, South Africa, Tanzania, Uganda, the Republic of Georgia, Armenia, Ukraine, Tanzania, and Myanmar.

She and her husband, Pastor Darryl, live in Missouri, enjoying the sweet life with their children and grandchildren.

Women Around the World
P.O. Box 29
Farmington, Mo. 63640

WomenAroundTheWorldMinistries.com
Email: waw@solidrockfamilychurch.org

Praise for

Women Around
the World

"Cindy and I have known Darlene for nearly 50 years. Her and Darryl's ministry has ministered to us and our congregation through these years. Darlene's ministry is empowering Women Around the World. We have witnessed her practical and dynamic teaching and training in places of the world where women have never been allowed to minister. The trust and confidence of the pastors, bishops and leaders is astounding! Whether a women's event or combined, she is received by all as a Mother in the Faith. She is like steel velvet—strong in Spirit, soft to the heart! She nurtures the Family of God but is a warrior in contending for truth. Freedom follows her, and wisdom abides. The favor of God, like that on Esther, is the point of reference we've seen. The results are undeniable, the fruit is remarkable, the transformations generational. Darlene is the reflection of her Father's love and grace. Commissioned by Christ and walking in the power of the Holy Spirit."

Pastors Danny & Cindy Wermuth
Joplin Family Worship Center
Joplin, Missouri

28234654R00094

Made in the USA
Lexington, KY
12 January 2019